Immigrant Son

Refusing to
Grow Up

Also by HARRY CHINCHINIAN:

Immigrant Son:
An Armenian Boyhood

~Essay/Autobiography

Pathologist in Peril

~Mystery

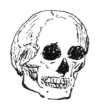

Murder in the Mountains

~Mystery

IMMIGRANT SON

Book Two

REFUSING TO GROW .. UP

Written and Illustrated

by

HARRY CHINCHINIAN

Plum Tree Press

Plum Tree Press
531 Silcott Road
Clarkston, Washington 99403

ISBN 0-9653535-6-7 (Soft Cover)
ISBN 0-9653535-7-5 (Hard Cover)

Library of Congress Catalog Card Number: 97-69993

9 8 7 6 5 4 3 2 1

Illustrations by author.
Layout and editing by Pine Orchard.
Cover design by Matt Gravelle.

All Plum Tree Press titles are distributed and publicized by:
Sheryn Hara & Company
P.O. Box 19732
Seattle, WA 98109
(425) 775-7868

Back cover photo of author during student days in Basel, Switzerland. Approximate English translation:
"I find happiness and peace in the mountains."

For Mary

Preface

Make new friends, but keep the old;
Those are silver, and these are gold.

—J. Parry

It was such an old-gold friend who said that he enjoyed what I wrote and asked me for more. So here's more with Book Two, *Immigrant Son: Refusing to Grow Up.*

I owe both of the *Immigrant Son* books to this friend, John Peterson, the banker, who chided and chided me for not washing my car.

It was my strong negative reaction to his kidding that made me think about the reason for not performing such a simple task. Trying to find the reason led to writing down some childhood inhibitions which I thought I had long forgotten and assumed their influence had diluted out over the years. Not so.

There are hundreds of stories similar to these that everyone has stored up. I know you have many of the same, and I hope you'll agree that there is always some basis for refusing to grow up.

—Harry Chinchinian

Lewiston, Idaho
Clarkston, Washington

Contents

1 Pop and America 1

2 Good-bye, Grocery Store 9

3 The Grocery Store Remembered 19

4 Camp 31

5 Nice Kids, Then Us 45

6 Hurry Up and Wait: The Infantry 59

7 College Begins 69

8 In the Mountains 83

9 Guilt and Former Chums 95

10 Medical School and Dr. Whipple 103

11 Marquette and Joe 117

12 Internship on the Wards 127

13 E.R. 137

14 Specializing 147

15 Pacific Northwest 159

16 Merry Mary 167

17 Failing 173

18 Teachers 183

1

Pop and America

1
Pop and America

"**N**O! WHY ARE YOU HAVING SO MUCH TROUBLE understanding no? Don't you understand what I'm saying?"

"Yes, with respect, I understand what you said," Pop replied.

For the *seventh* time, Pop had arrived at Ellis Island and was being turned away. The Immigration Officer recognized him and told him he wasn't wanted.

The officer was shaking his head. "Why don't you understand that? What will you do if I send you back?"

"Turn around and come back again on the next ship."

"And if I send you back again after that, what will you do?"

With respect, Pop politely answered, "Come back again."

The officer angrily swore, threw some papers around the desk, but finally let him into the United States, where he met Mom at Troy, New York.

Pop never did understand why the Immigration Officer let him in. Perhaps he knew Pop wanted to escape the terrible situation in Armenia where the Turks were in power. You see, the Christian Armenians had been almost annihilated by the Muslims during the time when Pop was growing up. So coming to America was not only a matter of survival, but also a journey of hope. Like many foreigners, he had heard this country was the most wonderful place on earth to live.

My pop's father, a wheat merchant, had taken him to other countries, and offered him a choice for a better life. But Pop heard, from talking to people in these different countries, explanations of how much better, according to their relatives, it was to live in America.

Pop made his choice, and luckily, his father had enough money to help him get on a ship from Marseille, France, to New York. And back again, over and over. *Seven* times!

Like many appreciative immigrants, Pop became a super-patriot. America was the sun, moon, and stars. She could do no wrong. The idea of anyone refusing military service, burning the flag, or doing anything against the government horrified him. He couldn't even tolerate the thought. How could you do something like that against America, the country you loved? Against the best country in the world? Cutting off your arms and legs would make more sense!

When I was younger, Pop kept telling me what a wonder this country was, and how lucky I was to be born

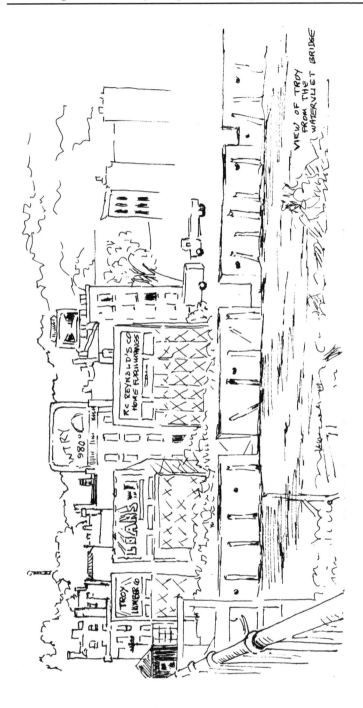

here. It didn't mean much to me then. He kept it up so often that it became a litany. Although we could tease him on any other subject, he would brook no teasing whatsoever on his opinion about the United States.

As I got older, I wanted to see for myself just how great America was. Being in the war gave me little time, even when I was in Europe, to see very much greatness. I couldn't make any comparisons since fraternizing with the enemy, even talking to them, was a court-martial offense. But when the war was over, I had the opportunity, thanks to the G. I. Bill, to get an education and travel anywhere in the world.

I studied French and German in college, went back to Europe, enrolled in foreign schools, and boarded with foreign families. I watched as they went through their daily lives, enjoying happy moments with them and suffering when they had sad times.

France was interesting, so was Germany, but Switzerland, where I lived as a student for a year and a half, was even more so. The Alps were truly breathtakingly beautiful mountains.

When you are in foreign countries, you adjust to their way of life and criticize nothing. As a guest, it's poor taste to do otherwise. It's only when you return home to America that you remember what other countries offered: rigid class structure, layers of suffocating regulations, enormous and unfair taxation systems defeating all but the most tenacious of entrepreneurs. You remember how the pioneer spirit was stifled by regulations which detailed how every business was allowed to operate, including the *hours* of operation. And if that wasn't enough, the different treatment of humans based on whether they're male or female, well . . . that remained incredible.

So after all this, what did I really learn?

Pop was right. America *is* the greatest country in the world.

2

Good-bye
Grocery Store

Tenth St and Oakwood Ave.

2

Good-bye, Grocery Store

BREATHLESSLY, AUNT MARY HURRIED into the grocery store. "Dick," she cried, "why are you shouting? Everyone can hear you down the block! What's wrong?"

"What's wrong? Is that what you ask? What's wrong?" screamed Uncle, his arms raised and his hands beseeching the heavens. "Here's my sister's boy who I took in off the streets through the kindness of my heart. I spent the best part of my life trying to show him how to run a business, thinking he'd appreciate it. Just when he gets old enough to be a help, what does he do?

"The ceiling or something falls on his head, making him crazy and he decides, all by himself, to make fancy pictures, which nobody wants to buy. For a living, he says! Who needs a crazy boy in a store?

"Hundreds of boys would pay for the chance I'm giving him and he's getting it free. So what does he do? He throws it back in my face and says he wants to draw pictures! And if that isn't crazy enough," Uncle bellowed, "he wants to go . . . play . . . FOOTBALL!"

"Football?" asked Aunt Mary, looking at me with her eyes widened in disbelief.

Well, all this started on a pleasant August evening. Feeling mellow, my uncle decided to talk to me about my future. He was worried that I was losing interest in being a storekeeper because I didn't even blink when he said he was going to leave the store to me.

When he died, that is.

But relatives never died. A lot of us were sons and nephews who worked for relatives, so I knew it was a regular thing to be told we were going to inherit the business. As far as we could see, it allowed the bosses to work us longer and harder for little or no pay.

Everyone else seemed to die, but bosses went on forever. In fact, we decided if people wanted to live a long time, they should become a boss of something, anything. It guaranteed long life.

It was one of those days when customers weren't coming in at all. Whenever that happened, Uncle Dick felt moody and often he'd light up a cigar. Puffing on the White Owl, he leaned on the marble counter and asked what I intended to do with my life. He expected me to say "storekeeper" as I had in the past.

In order to understand my answer, you have to realize that this was the era of N.C. Wyeth, Norman Rockwell, John Falter, John Clymer, and other great illustrators. They painted the covers of all the important magazines, and illustrated books and stories. They were the colossal greats of the time. At the impressionable age of sixteen, I replied to Uncle's question by saying I wanted to be an illustrator and maybe . . . a storyteller.

He choked on the smoke, coughed, and finally caught his breath. The words finally smoldered out of his mouth. "You already tell more stories than anyone wants to hear, so forget that. The stories you tell of why you're late for work—they already win prizes!

"What's that illus . . . mean? Is it drawing pictures? A fancy word for drawing pictures?"

"Yes," I answered meekly.

He was quiet for a moment, but the way his eyes squinted down meant trouble. It began with a suspiciously pleasant smile. "Tell me," he queried, "how many people draw pictures for sale?"

"In the United States?"

"Yes, in the United States!" he replied exasperated. "Where else do you intend to do this . . . drawing business? Ethiopia? It's a simple question: How many people draw pictures?"

"Probably 50 thousand," I guessed. And I added, "They're called artists."

"Artists? Artists? You call them what you will. I call them 50 thousand draw-ers." Uncle looked at me with narrowed eyes, took out a pencil, and sharpened it. "So," he said, as he wrote down the number 50,000, "tell me how many pictures each one can draw in a week that's not just good for the garbage can?"

I knew what was coming. I answered reluctantly,

"About three or four."

"Hmm . . ." thought Uncle out loud, wielding his sharpened pencil. "Twelve hours in a day, six working days in a week, and they only can make three or four pictures! They should work so hard! So 50 thousand lazy buggers each make four pictures for a total of 200 thousand pictures a week. Times 52 weeks in a year makes . . . let's see . . . 10 million 400 thousand. In ten years . . . never mind. How many of these sell?"

"I don't know. Not that many, I guess."

Uncle mimicked my words. "Not that many I guess." He raised his voice after blowing out a large puff of blue smoke. "Ten million drawings out there every year, year after year! One hundred million in ten years! And you want to make drawings and go into that kind of competition? Tell me, does anyone you know make a *living* at this drawing business?"

I had to admit I didn't know anyone.

Uncle nodded grimly. "So, you're saying you want to go into something you can't make a living at and all the time you're doing this, you want someone to feed you and keep clothes on your back."

"Um . . . Uncle?" I felt at this point that I should let *everything* out. The words came hesitantly, even though I had thought about telling Uncle for months and months. "I want to play football this fall when I go back to school."

The explosion was immediate.

"FOOTBALL? FOOTBALL? Now you have gone crazy!" Uncle began gagging on his words. Clearly this was too much. "First, picture drawing and now FOOT-BALL? What good is football going to do you when you're drawing pictures?"

"No good," I said. "I just want to get into some sort of sport. I'm a junior in high school, and it's now or never."

"Never is more like it!" Uncle's face was florid and his eyes bulged out so that the whites made a complete circle around the irises.

He shouted, "What good is football going to do you? What will you learn from it? You'll have bad knees and a bad back the rest of your life. For what?"

I answered as firmly as I could. "That's what I want to do."

That's when Uncle expanded his lungs and screamed, "Oh, my God. Oh, my God!" and that's when Aunt Mary came into the store and asked why Uncle was shouting.

"Football?" Her face became puzzled, looking at me with her eyes widened in disbelief. "Do you really want this?" she asked.

"Yes," I answered, careful not to look back at her directly. You see, Aunt Mary had the uncanny knack of being able to look into my eyes and guess what I was thinking, and I was afraid she might guess I wanted to meet girls.

Football players got to meet lots of girls. Cheerleaders especially. Even the bad players got to meet a lot of girls. I couldn't let my aunt know that. Then I'd really be in it deeper than I could ever get out.

Aunt Mary's presence pleased Uncle as did any audience. Again he raised his hands to the heavens and pleaded to what he knew was a just and sensible Deity. "Please, God!" he prayed. "Heal the mind of my sister's child. Take away his craziness!"

He looked at me and saw God had seen fit to deny him his request, at least right away, so he switched tactics. His voice penetrated through the thick smoke of the cigar.

He shouted, "Name someone you know—these picture makers you want to be like. They've got to be bums! Who else would be dumb enough to add to 10 million drawings a year?

"Football? I can show you lots of football players with bad backs and crippled legs. And now they can't do a decent day's work. Bums! You want to be a bum like them and live off working people?"

Aunt Mary tried to smooth it over. "Maybe he's just thinking about it because it's something different. Maybe . . . he'd like to take more pictures with the camera his cousin gave him? Maybe . . . he just wants some time off to watch those games they play at school."

Uncle looked at his wife with horror. *Time off?*

I knew what he was thinking: Nobody got *time off* in the grocery business. The store had to be kept opened. *Always.* What was she thinking?

I felt my voice tremble as I spoke, "I really have decided that I want to play football."

Uncle Dick lost control. He screamed, again looking to the heavens, "*Ahsvatz, Ahsvatz,* my God! No wonder You can't help him. His mind is completely gone. We're just looking at a body without any brain and at an open mouth that croaks nonsense."

"Now, now, Dickran," Aunt Mary said to her husband, "perhaps he's been sick." She stared at me carefully and asked, "Are you feeling all right, Harry?"

"Yes, Aunt Mary," I replied, "I'm fine. I really want to do this thing."

"Go home!" shouted Uncle Dick. "I'll talk to your mother and father. You can't work here and play football too. Make up your mind. Go! Get out of my sight! Come back when your brain is back in your body."

I picked up my jacket and left the grocery store.

Uncle's parting counsel was that I was not responsible for my actions since I was brain-dead; that drawing pictures and telling stories were not an honest or decent means of livelihood; and that I would end up in the county poorhouse with football knees, crippled, begging for whatever scraps of food some kind hearts would spare out of their own meager supply.

The worst of the worst, he told me, was that I had lost all sense of shame, because it didn't bother me that my poor family would have to make up a story to the neighbors on how my brain had suddenly gone "bye-bye."

3

The Grocery Store Remembered

3

The Grocery Store Remembered

Mom took the news poorly of my being fired and asked if I couldn't go back, for her sake, and apologize. When I said "no," she became teary-eyed because I had not only left a steady job, but also the nurturing care of her oldest brother. After all, didn't he teach me everything he knew—just as he promised? And hadn't he promised to leave me the store one day? What else could anyone possibly want in life, but to own a thriving business? Didn't I want to be a man of respect? Uncle couldn't read or write, but he was a man of respect.

At that time, I wished I could have relieved my mother's fears and bragged about something I had achieved or some special talent I had, but my chief success was failing at everything I tried to do. Running around with Antranik's gang was considered the opposite of achievement.

But Pop didn't seem to care about what happened to my job. He avoided being around people who were always in the middle of a major crisis. The constant shouting, screaming, and arm-waving, which Mom's side of the family seemed to do best, wore Pop down fast. I think he was secretly sympathetic about my leaving

Uncle's store and he smiled at me a lot when Mom wasn't looking, but he couldn't say anything.

The next weeks and months, Mom did what every well-meaning mother does. From the moment I got up until bedtime, she would constantly suggest alternative occupations. Unfortunately, there was actually a *Bishop* Chinchinian, so the priesthood was the first suggestion, also the second, the third, and the fourth.

Becoming a judge was thrown in as a diversion. She was reaching back in her mind to her days in the village where the Turks could do anything they wanted to the Christian Armenians, and the only one to stop them was a judge or lawyer who enforced the law and had the authority to punish.

Priests were never physically harassed, and judges provided law and order. Any other occupation was far less worthy. Drawing pictures was not even to be considered as an occupation. And football, well, playing football or any sports was a ridiculous waste of energy and time, which could be better put to productive use.

From the viewpoint of a sixteen-year-old, Uncle was a slave driver. He frowned on any sitting around. I had to keep busy and just looking busy wasn't enough. The floors had to be swept, the windows washed, the shelves and cans dusted. Coal and charcoal had to be put in ten-pound, twenty-five-pound, and fifty-pound bags, and their tops tied tightly. Every day some display had to be moved to a different location, and the price shaved a little if the product wasn't selling well.

My hours of work began right after school and lasted until the customers stopped coming into the store. Usually that was between 9:30 and 10:30 at night during the week. Saturdays, I opened the store at 7:30 in the morning and went home around 11:00 at night. Sundays, I opened at 8:00 A.M. and kept the store opened until midnight. The weekends were sort of a relief for my aunt and uncle. They were in and out, getting some rest from when I wasn't there.

If you told me that I was learning a work ethic by running a business and being responsible and such, I would have said you were crazy. Working in a store was the pits. If I made a single mistake, I was reminded of it over and over for weeks. Prison had to be better.

The way I saw it, customers came at the most inconvenient times. As soon as you climbed up a ladder, that's when a customer would come in. Or when your hands were really dirty from making bags of coal for sale, a customer would ask for ice cream to be scooped, which meant spending a lot of time washing carefully. Why couldn't customers ask me to pump gasoline or kerosene instead? It seemed they never did. Sure, and as soon as my hands were perfectly clean, that's when they would want a quart of oil put in their car. And as soon as my hands were dirty, that's when they decided they wanted crackers or sauerkraut out of the barrel. Couldn't they have ordered the food stuff first and *then* have me put the oil in the car?

Then the way they always came in at the same time.

Never singly. When it started to get dark or just about dusk, everybody seemed to decide to come to the store. It was *always* our busiest time.

And since Uncle sold wholesale cigarettes and candy to the other stores, I pulled a red wagon to deliver this merchandise. The wagon had its sides extended upward by a fence so it could hold more. No grocery was too far to travel to make a sale. Later, when I was older, I used a bicycle.

Would I miss working in a grocery store? Would I miss only being allowed to eat the crumbs and broken parts of newly shipped cookies from Nabisco? The cookie-cakes were shipped in large square boxes which we covered with a glass top. Each cookie, separated by a cardboard divider, looked like a beautiful jewel. There were layers and layers of them. Some were marshmallow and covered with chocolate, others had jelly centers, and others had hard vanilla or peanut butter fillings. All too few arrived broken and in crumbs. Eating just the cookie crumbs was dumb.

The partly spoiled banana or partly rotten apple or partly withered grapes in the cluster—that's what we salvaged. Only fruit that couldn't be sold could be eaten, and only cans with dents in them could be opened. When sandwiches were made, the twenty-nine-cents-a-pound bologna was to be eaten; the fifty-nine-cents-a-pound boiled ham was never to be touched. What's more, we were checked to make sure we were using mustard, not expensive mayonnaise.

Of course, my aunt and uncle followed all these rules, but it didn't impress me as anything but stupid, unreasonable, and real dumb. Once, I did catch Uncle cutting an extra slice of boiled ham for a customer and leaving it in the tray. Afterwards, when the customer had gone, he started to eat it and guiltily said, "Here. Have part of it. I cut a slice too much by mistake." Oh, that tasted so good!

Would I miss the serious scolding if I didn't know the price of something in the store? Or miss the daily interrogation about prices of goods and their mark-ups? "Haritoon, you've got to know your stock!" Uncle would say. The grocery store offered hundreds of things and nothing was marked as to price, so it wasn't easy.

If the store didn't have it, Uncle made sure it became available right away by sending me out for it. I was sent out, without notice, to other stores to purchase goods that we didn't have. We were never out—it was always in the "warehouse" and he expected me to come back with the right price for that too. If a customer asked for the same thing twice, it was put on order and became part of our regular stock so Uncle knew, from the wholesale price, if I paid too much to another grocer for an item.

Clearly, I felt put upon, working in the grocery store. A teen-ager doesn't see things from an adult's viewpoint. I didn't see how poor we were and how hard it was to make ends meet.

TEEN-AGER VIEW
OF UNCLE DICK.

I was cavalier about Uncle's feelings at the time, especially when he avoided speaking to me at family gatherings. Uncle felt he had spent all his time teaching me the basics of being a

ACTUAL VIEW OF UNCLE

storekeeper and I was paying him back by throwing it in the sewer, heading towards being a useless bum—drawing stuff nobody wanted and playing a stupid, brain-and-bone damaging game called football.

Of course, it took me quite a while to appreciate the rules Uncle taught me. He always started by saying,

"Haritoon, this is the *Number One Rule* . . . ." It took me but a short time to realize *all* his rules were Number One, especially the one I just forgot.

"Take care of the customer" meant *"please the customer."* Even the meanest and most difficult customers you tried to please, because they were the ones that usually talked the most about your store to other people. Taking care of the customers meant *their* needs came first, and if it interfered with anything you wanted to do at that moment, forget it.

That meant the opening and closing hours of the store were dictated by the customer. No matter how early or late, if a customer wanted something, then the store was "open." Even if it was closed, it was opened or would open pretty quickly. It meant greeting customers—every one of them—by name when they came in and saying their name again with a thank you when they left. It meant asking about those who were sick in the family and sending little gifts. Groceries were to be carried to the car, no matter how few or how busy we were.

Well, that was the easy part. The part I never understood was merchandising. For example, when Uncle had a good product on display at a reasonable price and it didn't sell, he would take it down, box it up in the back room for three months, then bring it out at a *higher* price. It sold out completely. "Just came in," he'd tell a customer. In a sense, I guess that was a correct statement—it "just came in" from the back room.

Another example with merchandising was the way

he sold something. He always started selling the highest priced item, even though it came in three price ranges: low, medium, and high. Uncle knew the customer could never afford the highest price. I would have understood this method if there was more profit in the higher priced one, but there wasn't. His explanation was that the customer was happier with the lower price if you started with the most costly. I guess it was like pricing a Rolls-Royce, then a Cadillac, and then a plain Ford to customers. They were glad they could pay for the Ford.

Uncle bought lots of Christmas candy, the hard, boiled type that kept forever. He'd put the candy in the window and on the counters because it dressed up the place—it was so pretty and colorful, formed in different shapes: ribbons, canes, ovals, and squares. He liked the long ribboned candy best. Right after Christmas, he would put the candy on sale at half-price. But during Christmas, he had doubled the price, so afterwards, he ended up with the regular price anyway.

Another merchandising trick was to leave something dusty and dirty in the window. When someone complained about it, Uncle would agree with the customer, compliment him on his sharp eyes, suggest that the dirt was only on the outside of the box or that the clothing could be washed like new, and offer to sell it at a discount. They'd dicker about the price, and the customer would walk away happy at finding a bargain. Uncle would wait a few days and then place something else that was "soiled" in another window for a customer to discover.

The grocery business taught you about people and how to judge them quickly because a lot of people wanted things on credit. You learned, after being stiffed a few times, that the more someone talked, the less likely they were to be genuine. Uncle didn't believe written recommendations about anybody. He insisted on a quick phone call to someone *he* knew as a check on the person's character. His friends had their own network which was as quick and efficient as any computer. He said that only important, bad things about a person would be told to you face to face or over the telephone. Those nice letters didn't mean anything and were meant to be read only by the person who carried them around.

It wasn't until years later that I could appreciate what I learned in the grocery store. The work ethic didn't seem so important back then. All teen-agers think of long working hours as a jail sentence. The grocery store was *dumb*. My work was *dumber*. And my uncle was *dumb*, *dumb*, *dumb*!

For example, "What business are you in?" was one of Uncle's favorite questions. I hated . . . no, *despised* being asked that question because it was always followed by a long lecture, even when I gave the required answer, "Pleasing the customer."

"*Number One Rule*," he would say, looking very serious, "*Number One Rule*." Then he'd go into fine detail about how everyone talks about *listening* to the customer, but you can't trust what the customer *says* he wants. You watch what he actually *does* and what he buys!

What was that again? Please customers but don't listen to what they say? Instead, carefully watch what they do and especially what they buy? What a confusing bunch of garbage! Can you imagine how hard it was for a teenager not to listen to a word of what people said?

It wasn't until I had to go out among strangers and try to earn a living that I understood the value of his wisdom, especially about being there and being available. Once you're competing, it does help to get up earlier and leave later than anyone else—just as we did with the store, opening earlier and closing later than the other storekeepers.

Remember that amusing saying, "The longer and harder I work at something, the luckier I get"? Well, in my life it seemed to work out just that way.

All these lessons, which I found useful and which are now taught in graduate business schools, came from a small corner grocery store—from an immigrant uncle, who never learned to read or write.

4

camp

4
Camp

W E SHOULD NEVER HAVE BEEN ALLOWED into a nice camp
with nice kids. How did we get in? Antranik.

I thought I saw the last of our gang leader when he
stopped showing up for school, but he was always near
the action or right in it. It was fun to watch how he oper-
ated because he had the natural ability of a con man and
could shift gears, look bashful and embarrassed at the
same time, and in his own funny way, talk with a silver
tongue. He didn't use this "charm" with us because if he
wanted something, he just took it. One punch and you
learned to give it up quicker the next time. Sweet-talk-
ing us would have been a waste.

Antranik learned, maybe from watching Pastor Perry
and Miss Cass, that he could have a special niche in life
and that was making ministers and priests feel guilty for
not doing something for a poor, down-in-his-luck, deserv-
ing person who never whined, and who was trying to do
right but needed a helping hand. Through a Methodist
Church function, he met some ministers who offered him
a job in the kitchen at summer camp and he immediately
invited three of us to go along—without permission, of
course.

Antranik took me along because I looked like one of

the nice camp kids with my big shock of black curly hair, ready smile, and innocent look. It wasn't "innocent" so much as dumb, but so what, I was glad to get away from the hot city. Of course, it was accepted that Antranik would get half of anything we received in the line of tips or gifts. That meant anything and everything. And if there was one thing you didn't do with Antranik, it was to hold out on him. When he said half, he meant at least half. Once in a while, he took it all and then gave most of it back the next day. It was his idea, I guess, to let you know who the boss was.

The camp grounds and buildings actually belonged to the Y.M.C.A. and were located on a large lake more than a dozen miles north of Troy. It was leased out to religious groups a few weeks before and a few weeks after the Y's own regular camping time.

When we arrived at camp after walking miles on the dirt road, which was a long way from the main highway, we were told to go away. Antranik didn't say anything, just tossed his head to one side, meaning go behind the kitchen, which we did. Right away he had us working like crazy, cleaning things up. When bosses saw how hard we were sweating and working without a break, they stopped telling us to go home. Maybe they needed somebody to do the grunt work like wash dishes, wait on tables, and clean up. Or maybe they really thought they'd improve our way of life.

We sure weren't much good for anything else in camp because none of us could swim or teach things like crafts

or hiking or boating or anything about nature. In spite of those drawbacks, I like to think we did teach the kids something permanent, even though it wasn't anything close to what their parents wanted.

We started two weeks before the regular camp, and kids from eight to eighteen years of age were accepted. They had their own name for the nondenominational camp which meant they wanted a lot of kids from different churches to sign up. They promised the parents there would be lots of talks on how the campers should live their lives by following the Bible's teachings. From what we saw, these kids came from nice parents who wanted their kids to improve themselves, associate with their own class or a better class of people, and avoid the rotten types who ran around in gangs, like us.

Well, they couldn't have found anyone better than Antranik to appreciate nice kids from nice families. He went out of his way to get to know them. You could tell from a block away when he met one, because he lit up like a Christmas tree. His face turned different colors of bright red, and he began this funny smile of his with the droopy lower lip. Soon, his friendly arms would wrap around the kid as though they were best buddies. He would admire the shirt, the coat, the pants with the deep pockets, and the handsome shoes. And it'd be a matter of short time that Antranik would be wearing a couple things the kid once had on. The nice kid assumed Antranik just wanted to "try it on" or just wear it for a few minutes.

Sometimes we'd watch money change hands, as a loan, of course, from the nice kid to Antranik because the nice kid's new friend was real bad off and had to have a couple dollars right then for medicine that his mom needed. Who could refuse to lend a few dollars to a guy for his sick mom if you had it in your pocket? What are friends for—and it was just for a few hours, right?

"Pay back right away. Promise."

If you couldn't take advantage of nice guys, who could you take advantage of? By being born nice, they were asking for it, weren't they?

The ministers were there to guide and to demonstrate the practice of true Christian ethics especially to the counselors, some of whom, they hoped, would enter the ministry. "Leadership through God's Commandments" they called it or something like that, and the ministers really tried to get the counselors to run things. This is where we came in because the counselors' faith and abilities had to be tested by someone, sometime, so we helped them, in all kinds of ways, by taking on the burden of testing them.

A few counselors weren't ready for this leadership business because they tried to act strict and stern like their own parents did, but it didn't work and they ended up getting real upset over everything, and the ministers had to take over without acting as though they were taking over.

Antranik was never without his Bible and passed himself off as the chef's assistant. He never got enough food

at home to eat and was always hungry, so this was a perfect job for him. Even though the rest of us weren't invited, we were lucky that the chef was lazy and made us do everything. We'd never done anything in the kitchen before, but we were kept there to help him anyway.

The first night, the chef had a little too much to drink and happily told us to follow these rules: for the first three days of camp, the meals had to be great so that everybody would write home good things about the food. After that, he said he didn't sweat it until the last three days of camp when he'd really put out the great stuff again, like steaks and things, and make everyone think, especially the visitors, that it was this way the whole time.

It didn't take long for Antranik to take charge of the kitchen because the cook had more than a little weakness for drink, and Antranik made certain the cook never ran out of it. Of course, liquor of any type was forbidden in camp and the Dutch Reform Directors were especially death on any form of alcohol. I had the idea, from listening to the directors, alcohol was made by the Devil himself in his own personal factory.

We did our jobs right, like peel spuds, slice carrots and onions and cucumbers, and fry the hamburgers. Antranik was a different person, ordering us around and telling us to work harder and harder, especially when anyone in authority was listening. He kept carrying the Bible everywhere and nodding when he met anyone. It wasn't odd to hear him using words like "Bless you, brother," because that's what he often said just before he punched you, even though his "Amen" blessing still hurt the worst.

We made lots and lots of mashed potatoes with gravy, and for dessert the cook taught us how to make a fancy bread pudding with stale bread and Jell-O vanilla pudding mix. The fancy part was throwing in some raisins and nuts. We thought adding such a twist was pretty high-class eating, even though we never tasted bread pudding before. We tried improvements by adding chocolate chips and peanut butter. But when we put them both in at the same time and the whole batch turned into a scorched blob that could hardly be scraped out of the burnt pan, we had to go back to the first way.

Antranik liked corn more than anything else, so we had lots of corn—at every lunch and every dinner. If people complained, they got it in their mashed potatoes too or mixed up in their salads. Except for that and for trying to put peanut butter on everything when he ran out of ideas, Antranik didn't do too badly with the kids.

The cook, after a few days with no limit on liquor, insisted on becoming soused around the clock, then loudly gave his opinion of ministers in general, which was not very high. So we had to protect him, when he was drunk, from being overheard by anyone, especially the prissy-type counselors.

When he was sober, the cook was a jolly man and enjoyed talking to everybody, especially the ministers' ladies. He went way out of his way to chat with them.

One afternoon, he escaped from our guarding him and wandered up the dirt road in front of the faculty cabins where he met a young, pretty Dutch Reform minister's wife who took his question of their doing something intimate together all too seriously. She right away told her husband and he confronted the cook, only to have the cook, pleasantly enough, ask for details about the minister's sex life.

Without letting him pack his clothes and gear or say good-bye, the cook was in the back seat of the Ford between two ministers while another one drove. The three ministers had such grim faces that they looked like they had latched onto the Devil himself and were going to torch his factory. As soon as they thought they were out of earshot, they began yelling at the poor cook and told him to turn his head away from them because the smell of liquor was too overpowering and stank so badly.

As a result of the cook leaving, Antranik was asked if he could handle the kitchen, which Antranik said he would try hard to do and "thank you for the great honor." Everybody, except the ministers, knew he had been doing it all anyway. Only now, it was going to be easier since Antranik didn't have to sneak in all the booze for the cook, and we had more free time because we didn't have to spend it all on guard duty.

A lot of counselors began to depend upon Antranik for relief from their schedule. The ministers had every minute of the day booked solid from the moment the campers got up to when they went to bed. So the counselors particularly liked being invited to the kitchen at night after the campers were asleep, and liked getting all they wanted to eat and drink.

We played cards and threw dice just for the sport of the game, not for winning money. Antranik insisted that these were games of sport and not gambling. Anyone who said we were doing anything but playing and having fun was going to have to answer to him. We were definitely not playing for money, even though, in a few days, Antranik had I.O.U.'s or had cleaned the money out of just about every counselor who came in for the free drinks and food.

Antranik heard, somehow, that a group of girls were camping across the lake. He talked the counselors into visiting the girls while the ministers were having their nightly inspirational prayer meeting, which usually lasted about an hour and a half. They bribed one counselor to take charge of the campers, then all of us took off in canoes and boats. I went in Antranik's rowboat with the kitchen crew.

The girls were surprised and screamed when we arrived, but it didn't take them long to get dressed up and invite us inside the cabin. There were ten of us and six of them. The oldest girl in charge named Marlene wore purple lipstick. I'd never seen purple lipstick before and couldn't take my eyes off her. One of the counselors asked me which girl was the prettiest and I said the older girl named Marlene.

He went up and imitating my voice, told her I thought she was "bee . . . yoo . . . ti . . . ful." She liked the sound of that and came up to me and asked me to repeat it, so I did.

"Bee . . . yoo . . . ti . . . ful."

She smiled and said too bad I wasn't a lot older. The other counselors tried to take off on that comment because they were a lot older, but she just smiled. I sure wished I was a lot older.

Antranik quick-like found a girl who was exactly his type and soon was talking up a storm. The oldest counselor tried to find out more about the girls and what they were doing all by themselves in a rented cabin on the lake, but they wouldn't say anything more than they came to have fun. The oldest in charge, Marlene, wouldn't let the girls give out any more than their first names. Even the smoothest and best-looking counselor told us later he had to sneak back three times just to get Marlene's address.

We got booted out of the cabin by Marlene after awhile and it was a good thing because by now, the ministers' meeting should have been close to being over. The counselors took off in the canoes and paddled like mad towards camp.

When we arrived, all the ministers were there with flashlights, waiting on the dock and on shore.

Two guys in a canoe tried to sneak away by going down the shoreline and head back later on foot, but the ministers had counted the canoes that were gone and kept looking. Finally, the ministers caught them in the light of their flashlights and made them turn back by calling out their names. They told the counselors they were very disappointed in their actions.

None of the counselors squealed as to the real reason why they took the canoe rides, except to say they needed to get away, which wasn't strictly a lie, I guess, but not exactly the truth either, all of which made me feel better about them because they were normal guys after all.

When the ministers spotted us in the rowboat, they didn't even help us land in the dark, or tell us they were disappointed in us, which would have been a nice thing to do because we "needed to get away" just like the counselors did. It made us feel left out when none of them said they were disappointed in us. I suppose disappointments were reserved for campers and counselors only.

Anyway, the reason they ended up out there looking for all of us was because they canceled their inspirational prayer meeting. I still don't think ministers should do things like that—set up regular schedules for themselves like prayers and such, and then cancel them for no reason or no warning to the rest of us.

5

Nice kids, Then Us

5
Nice Kids,
Then Us

AFTER THAT NIGHT across the lake, one of the ministers thought too many counselors were being influenced by Antranik instead of by true Christian fellows like himself, since the counselors were beginning to talk funny like Antranik, use his way of talking, and worst yet, laugh like him.

But there wasn't anything quoted from Antranik that could be criticized because Antranik was always quoting the Bible, the book he was never without. If a minister came in to talk to Antranik about something, Antranik would pick up the Bible and ask the minister some questions about it that he didn't understand. As the minister got deeper and deeper into the explanation, Antranik's face would get more and more serious, and he would act like he was concentrating hard on every word the minister was saying. But when Antranik could sneak a look at me, he'd twitch his eye. It wasn't a wink, but a very close brother to it.

It didn't take long for most ministers to steer clear of the kitchen or run in to say something and run out right away, insisting they were late for a meeting.

The Bible Student
Rebuffed.

Well, this one minister felt that Antranik's type of character was not what he wanted to see imitated. Not at all. So he decided to let Antranik know what was what and who ran the camp.

Now, our busiest time was just before putting supper on the table—you know how things get hurried so everything can be delivered nice and hot. But that's when this minister decided to corner Antranik in the kitchen and explain, in careful detail, how and when things should be done. Antranik was to stay in the kitchen, not to talk to any of the campers and counselors, and to do his work better.

The minister finished by stating that supper was always fifteen minutes late and that this type of delay was no longer going to be tolerated, and asked if Antranik understood.

Well, Antranik gratefully agreed with everything he was being told and promised to do better, and he thanked the minister for taking time from his busy schedule to explain so much that Antranik had been wondering about, ever since he began. It was a joy among joys, Antranik concluded, to meet a minister who cared enough to want to do things the *best* way, which was always the *right* way, and did the good reverend have time to go through the Bible with him sometime? Anytime? The minister glared without saying yes or no . . . and then left.

When supper was finally served thirty minutes late because of this delay, the same minister found cayenne pepper in his soup, cayenne pepper in his salad, cayenne pepper in his meat, and cayenne pepper in his vegetables. After one bite of each, the minister screamed, jumped up, brought the food back to Antranik, complaining bitterly about it, which was a mistake because Antranik, in front of the whole camp, picked up a fork, put one bite after another from the minister's plate into his own mouth and stared at the minister the whole time without blinking.

"I'm sorry, Reverend," said Antranik, "I don't understand what you're complaining about. It's good food with little seasoning. See? Here. Look. I've eaten almost all of it. Does anyone else at your table have any such complaint? No? How come?"

The minister's mouth flew open and he didn't know what to say. He was so mad and intent on screaming about his food that he didn't think to offer any of it to his fellow

ministers, so they could back him up about the hot pepper. What threw him off was the innocent way Antranik
ate almost the entire plate right in front of the whole camp
without blinking, to show it was all right.

All he could do was glare hard at Antranik, with his
mouth closing and opening, trying to say something.
When he got back his speech, it was too late to ask anyone else to sample anything because Antranik's fork had
dirtied the whole plate. Besides, all the food had disappeared into the garbage with the slops. We took charge
right after that, while Antranik disappeared in the back
kitchen to drink gallons of ice water.

The rest of the evening, the minister was bitter about
how stupid he looked in front of everybody and how
Antranik made a fool of him in front of the whole camp
and how the campers laughed about it. He made lots of
bad comments about Antranik's cooking, most of them
extra loud so Antranik could hear. It was good he didn't
know that Antranik, right then, was occupied with throat
and stomach troubles, and couldn't hear the comments
about his cooking. But Antranik was told what the minister said soon afterwards.

That night, the minister woke up sneezing and sneezing, and couldn't stop. His pillow tasted like cayenne
pepper. He insisted that the pepper was inside, mixed up
with the feathers, and that the pillow had to be thrown
away, even though he couldn't actually see or find any
pepper. The next morning, once again, he began the terrible sneezing when he drove his car. It happened every

time he got in to drive. He tried to tell everyone (that is, anyone who would listen) that someone had sprinkled cayenne pepper on the floor mat, under the seat of his car, and in the ducts, right where the fresh air came in. The counselors began calling him "Hot Pepper" but being the kind of person he was, he didn't see anything funny about the nickname at all.

When the campers found how mad it made the minister when the words "hot pepper" were said, they all said it, just to bug him, which is something you shouldn't do in a Christian camp. I mean, teasing was all right, but bugging was pretty close to unfriendly, if it wasn't exactly unfriendly.

For Antranik's part, he looked innocent when "pepper" kept being brought up in conversations, and so the next grocery list for needed supplies from town included an order for cayenne pepper. Antranik explained he would like to try to cook with some and see for himself how that particular pepper tasted, since everybody seemed to be talking about it.

After that, things settled down, so it was now time to help the good campers who really needed us.

It was simple to work with the nice kids who came to camp. I mean just take the fact that they weren't allowed to stay out late at night, or as late as they wished. Just that alone made them easy to take advantage of and scare.

When things go Slurp! Gurp! and Grrrrrr! in the night, that's when you need a friend. And that's where we came in. Everybody's friend, we were, and we were always there when needed.

Of course, in order to make it work, we had to have stuff that went Slurp! Gurp! and Grrrrr! at the right time and better still, bugs that crawled in beds and took bites.

Kids who never had leeches on their bodies really panicked. There were lots of those small black things in the lake. They worked best whenever it rained—thunder and lightning helped—because the roof leaked easily and if it didn't, we made sure it did, in the right spots.

Another thing: there's something about getting wet, scared, and bit by something in the dark that strains a kid more. No guy wanted to be known as a bed-wetter. Anyone who did *that* was a sissy and a Momma's boy. It was surprising how many kids actually believed they had wet the bed and how much they would pay us not to tell the other campers. The trick was to make sure it was genuine and warm, and not just plain water. And you know, we just so happened to have a continual, abundant supply of that. The genuine, warm stuff, I mean.

Camp was only half through, and we noticed the kids were getting more and more bored. They were sick of talks about sin and resisting temptation. Each talk had lots and lots of sin in it and ended the same way: "You should imitate godliness in every thought and deed." Heck, the kids deserved some relief and we decided to show them how to get it.

So to get started, we picked a few campers we trusted to keep their mouths shut, no matter what. At first, they were terribly slow in learning how to liven up the camp.

But after plugging up the septic tank to get everything backed up and stinking, they were ready for anything since all the Christian lessons got canceled for a whole day, which they thought was terrific fun.

It helped Antranik too, in a strange way. It convinced anyone who had doubts about him, that he was a self-sacrificing, rough-cut, shining jewel. Didn't they see with their own eyes how he walked into all that filthy muck, found the problem, shoveled it, cleaned it out, fixed it, and didn't even want to be thanked for what he did? And he did this after none of the ministers or counselors would volunteer.

The campers liked having something exciting happen. They wanted to do the same thing again, right away, but anybody knows you don't pull the same stunt twice like that without getting caught. You see how much we had to teach them?

Next, we showed the campers how to put food coloring in the water supply. They argued about whether red, green, or blue was best. They decided blue drinking water tended to turn people off most and they were right. More of their Christian lessons were canceled, so some other meetings could be held as to what to do about the contamination. A guy from the health lab in Troy was called to come out and take samples. He said to boil the water for five minutes, which is what we thought he'd say, so we got busy in the kitchen and boiled huge pots of water.

After that, the water supply ran dry and no one could

understand the reason . . . the camp bell disappeared into the woods and wasn't found until later so schedules weren't exactly on time . . . a whole lot of grasshoppers were let loose in the dining hall while everybody was eating . . . some snakes were found in beds, even though they were just small garter snakes . . .

But we were running out of time. Camp was ending. During the last three days, Antranik followed the advice of the disgraced cook and had us work like crazy putting out the most terrific meals he could think of putting together. He even tried to get in good with the parents by giving them free dinners when they came to pick up their kids, but the directors insisted on collecting twenty-five cents from each parent.

Somebody squealed about Antranik playing cards with the counselors at night and having liquor in the pantry. Sure enough, some ministers spied through the window and saw the card playing. Three of them came in through the back door and the "Hot Pepper" minister came in from the dining room door.

The ministers took over bossing everyone around, and the counselors were shoved aside and not even asked their opinions, which I still don't think was right because they did tell the counselors they were the leaders in charge. I mean, how can you put someone in charge one minute and take their responsibility away the next? In fact, they told the counselors to go to bed.

Then they grabbed up the cards and, worse yet, searched the pantry and found a bottle of opened liquor.

It didn't matter that the cards were just a sporting game, or that a surprised Antranik tried to tell them the liquor was left over when the cook disappeared so suddenly and wasn't able to collect his belongings.

"Honest," he said, "ask anyone. Smell my breath." But they wouldn't.

I think they had their minds made up before they even came into the kitchen, because they told Antranik since he was in charge of the kitchen, anything that happened in it was his responsibility. What's more, considering such shameful circumstances, he was lucky to be allowed to stay, but he should realize he was not to be invited back next year.

He wasn't. And so we weren't either.

I've got to finish by telling you how much I've always envied nice kids, especially these nice kids in camp. You see, I wouldn't know how nice kids think and act. They're still a mystery, because I spent most of my time looking at the world through the cracks of the coal cellar door. I could write a chapter on thoughts I had as a kid hunkered down in the coal bin. Lots of chapters, actually, because that's where I was put when I got too much for them at home and too much for relatives when we went to visit.

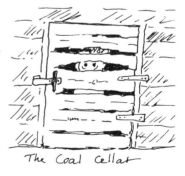

The Coal Cellar

The coal cellar was a favorite punishment of Aunt Pemi, who had a huge garden with lots and lots of fruit trees. I was hardly there five minutes when she'd get mad at me, and send me down to the cellar and lock me in.

Once, she forgot that she put me in her coal cellar early in the morning, and it wasn't until dark that she remembered. Thinking I was dying, dead, or worse, she hobbled down the steps, shouting, *"Ahnoosh Haritoon, Ahsvatz.* Sweet Harry, oh God," and all the time praying that nothing had happened.

When she opened the door, there I was, sitting on the coal pile, my face covered with black anthracite dust, looking tired, sleepy, and sad.

She cried her apologies, hugged and hugged me, and gave me all kinds of nuts, *leblebboo,* and sweets, including a string of walnuts that had been covered with thickened, hard, dried grape juice. It was great. For a week afterwards, she gave me any sweet that I wanted—even filled my pockets with them.

She never thought I would do something like escape from the cellar by lifting the simple latch, play outside all day, and then, as soon as I heard her footsteps, run back into the cellar and wait. Or cover my face with coal dust. Or look tired and sleepy and sad when, in truth, I'd just finished an all-day fight with the neighbor kids, wrestling, punching, and slinging the half-rotted plums and peaches from her orchard at them.

No. She knew I wouldn't do something like that.

After all, I did learn true Christian ethics at the Fifth Avenue Methodist Church and a lot more great stuff working under Antranik at a nondenominational religious camp, and wouldn't, no, couldn't do something like that.

Or even *think* to do something like that.

6

Hurry Up and Wait: The Infantry

6

Hurry Up and Wait: The Infantry

WELL, I PLAYED FOOTBALL and enjoyed it. Better still, I got to know a few girls, learned to dance, and shortly afterwards found a job in a meat market next to the railroad tracks in downtown Troy. Because of the shorter hours, no Sundays or holidays, my school grades improved, although I admit they only went from stink to poor. Still, an improvement was an improvement.

After me, brother Leo started working for Uncle but left (for about the same reasons I left) to work in another grocery in South Troy. He took me to the Y.M.C.A. and had me join. The first thing I did was stay under the hot showers for an hour. He laughed and said he did the same thing at first.

The Y had a swimming pool, weightlifting equipment, and a summer camp on Burdette Lake. I met Morey Paine, the Boy's Director, who invited me to come to camp. I accepted, hoping none of the ministers who came around would remember me as Antranik's helper.

I needn't have worried. My height was changing so fast with the swimming and weightlifting, that they probably wouldn't have recognized me anyway. And I wasn't going to bring it up.

Under Morey Paine, camp was completely different from how I knew it. Morey knew how to have fun running a camp with the kids. Happily, we hammered, lifted, painted, fixed, mended, and patched. Soon all the boats, canoes, and camp buildings were repaired.

I stayed on as an assistant of sorts. Each summer, I was invited to return and worked up to counselor, then program manager, and eventually waterfront director. The daily boating, canoeing, hikes, and calisthenics were actually a paid vacation. The constant swims led to obtaining my Senior Life Saving Certificate.

All these activities helped a great deal in basic Army training when I was drafted at eighteen into the Infantry in September, 1944. I had never been out of Troy, New York, until the Army sent me to Fort Dix, New Jersey; Fort McClellan, Alabama; Fort Meade, Maryland; Camp Miles Standish, Massachusetts; then overseas on a Liberty Ship.

During basic infantry training, we learned a lot of things that made life easier. One was that any question we asked was dumb, except asking when we were going to eat. And even that was dumb if it was asked right after we ate, or right after we were handed boxes of K or cans of C rations.

For one thing, asking a question irritated the officers and sergeants. For another, asking a question pulled you out of the crowd and put a mark on your helmet. The next time an officer needed someone for latrine duty, or re-digging the latrine ditch, or for KP, or scrubbing garbage cans, or guarding prisoners, or demonstrating something, which was the same as serving as a bad example, the officer remembered—guess who?

Another thing we learned early in basic training, was that officers were not your buddies. Officers came in all sizes and shapes, just like foot soldiers, but they had *authority*, which meant any question of their orders and they could have you placed under court martial, which meant the stockade, which meant they weren't your buddies and weren't going to be your buddies—ever.

Also during training, we learned quickly that when an officer said, "I need a volunteer," it was the same as saying, "I need a sap." You never, never volunteered because there weren't *any* good jobs in the infantry.

The best officers just tried to do their job, get the job done, and head for home. They handled their job by having soldiers line up and count off. The even numbers got the work that day, and the odd numbers received the same work the next day. It was fair.

Dangerous officers were ones that didn't know enough to be scared. There was no one scarier than that. They didn't last long—either they got shot or went bananas.

Actually, the scariest officers were those who *believed* in exactly interpreting President Roosevelt's speeches. Their firm beliefs were: (1) the December days of Pearl Harbor would go down in infamy and never be forgotten; (2) the Germans were the scourge of the earth; (3) the

Japanese were vermin and had to be exterminated; (4) the Russians were our good friends; and (5) all the rest of the fluff.

It's impossible to work for leaders who are out of contact with reality and who try to follow *exactly* what the Standard Operating Procedure (S.O.P.) Manual states for each and every occasion. These misguided officers honestly felt in the marrow of their bones that if it wasn't covered by the Manual, then the situation didn't exist. There was no use arguing with someone who truly believed that generals knew best, any more than it was arguing with a child about the tooth fairy. These officers traded the real Bible for the Army's bible, and whatever was written in it, was Absolute.

A few officers thought they found a niche in the Army that they could exploit and began to look for ways to get promoted, which meant we had to make them look good by doing things that could get us all easily killed. But even these self-promoters weren't as bad as those who "went by the book." At least the promoters wanted to survive and had the future in mind.

Well, the first day of being in enemy territory cleared our brains. After that, we expected to get one dumb order after another from our officers and we weren't disappointed.

"Run out in the street and see if you draw enemy fire. Don't worry, we'll back you."

Sure. Oh, yeah. Well, we learned the best answer to that: "Let's both go and both be heroes together, lieutenant. I don't want to hog all the glory."

The foot soldier specializes in marching with rifle and full backpack and that's what we did. We marched and marched and all too seldom, were trucked, through France, Belgium, and Germany.

Once, in France, we thought we were in heaven when we rode in their "40 and 8" railroad cars for a short distance. For this event, speed was necessary but so was evasive action of troop movements, because it was January, 1945, and we were being rushed up to stem the Battle of the Bulge, which was the last gasp of the enemy.

As soon as we arrived in Aachen, Germany, without sleep or rest, we were put on guard duty, around the bivouac area of our camp. It was enemy territory, and they had recently finished the bombing. Except for the light from the flames, the night was pitch black. Foul smoke spread everywhere from the rubble. Bullets continually pinged around us—snipers practicing on free targets, even though the city had surrendered. We were warned not to make a sound because that's what the snipers wanted.

I couldn't see or hear the other guard and he couldn't hear or see me, so there was no back-up. Worse yet, they didn't give us time to sight in our M1's for accuracy. How was I going to shoot back and hit anything?

I was so cold, so tired, so hungry, and so scared that I ended up in a fury of the-hell-with-it-all and told myself that if a sniper hadn't picked me off and I was still alive at daylight, nothing would be able to scare me again the rest of my life.

From that moment on, I knew how we should handle ourselves in the infantry. It's as though you begin to play a game according to the rules and find everything screwed up. Once you understand that the game is ruled by continued confusion and disorder, then you can work things out. If you read about the history of wars and screw-ups, let me assure you, it's a hundred times more disorganized than anyone can record. Especially with what the foot soldier had to do.

So, you see, we had to take care of each other in spite of what the officers told us to do, and still not deliberately disobey an order. You couldn't put them in a position of having to say, "That's an order, soldier!" We used our innate charm and will to stay alive, by not doing anything too stupid. When the enemy was already beaten and retreating, "Hell, why hurry? Give 'em a little time."

After several months of advancing from city to city through Germany, in which one rubble looked like another, we were told to slow up and wait. It seemed we waited for weeks, letting the Russians confiscate more and more German territory, an idea from the State Department that we should make the Russians look good. A lot of orders came from the State Department and they were obeyed.

From a second story window in Leipzig, we watched the meeting and exchange of gifts between the Russians and General "Lightning Joe" Collins. Lightning Joe gave the Russian general a beautiful, shiny Jeep and, in return, received a rifle.

My mind, still that of a grocery store trainee, couldn't help interpreting that gesture as not much of a return gift after the Russians insisted we mark time so they could get credit for capturing hundreds of miles of German territory. Still, it was an exciting day because with that, the war was officially over in Europe for us. The foot soldier was no longer needed.

We were still at war with Japan, but the rules stated that soldiers would receive a mandatory thirty-day furlough if they were to be sent to a different theater of operations. The thirty days home went quickly. Then after our visit home, we were sent by train to various staging areas in California: Camp San Luis Obispo, Fort Ord, Presidio of Monterey, and San Francisco.

Orders for embarkation kept being delayed without any reason. When the atom bombs were dropped, we knew why. The rule of a thirty-day furlough between theaters was just enough time delay to keep us from being shipped overseas. Japan surrendered and I was now in a non-essential category, so I was honorably discharged from the Army as a staff sergeant.

Years later, I would appreciate the true hero of World War II. It was not the flamboyant Patton, or the self-serving MacArthur, or the popular Eisenhower, or any other man or woman about whom we were given glowing reports in the field.

The true hero was General George C. Marshall, the one soldier who had not only intellect, but vision and moral character.

Although Roosevelt and Churchill made policy and often quarreled about their conflicting ideas, General Marshall patiently and diplomatically took their more sensible ideas and turned them into strategy. He was not only the single most valuable person in winning the war; but afterwards as well, when he helped the war victims with the Marshall Plan, he was the most valuable statesman in keeping peace.

Like many true heroes, he was so self-effacing that history recognizes his contribution all too little. No doubt about it, General Marshall was the neglected giant of World War II.

Now, with the war ended, by the age of twenty years, I had been given free travel through New Jersey, Alabama, Maryland, Massachusetts, Colorado, and California. In addition, I had marched, even though it was with rifle and heavy backpack, in Scotland, England, France, Belgium, and Germany.

The trip through the United States was great; but the European travel, all free admittedly, left me with only repressed memories and remembrances always of being worried, cold, and hungry and of other times being hungry, cold, and worried.

One thing that has stood by me is the anger in Aachen, Germany, at being so poorly equipped, disoriented, and without back-up: Nothing has ever scared me since.

Nothing.

1

College Begins

7
College
Begins

AFTER MY DISCHARGE FROM THE ARMY, I came back two years wiser, only to work in a flour mill loading freight cars. I hoped to go to college someday, but didn't have any incentive. Then, I found out that the G.I. Bill offered to pay tuition, books, and subsistence. Four years? Everything paid? No strings? Wow! So when I heard about a local college wanting to teach veterans, I enrolled.

I started at Russell Sage in Troy, New York, and went to Union College in Schenectady; then to Middlebury College, Vermont; Colby College, Maine; Universtaet Basel, Switzerland; and the University of Colorado at Boulder where they pushed me out with a B.A. degree.

Russell Sage College, a girl's school, accepted veterans for one year with the clear understanding that we were to go to school only at night and that we wouldn't mingle with the day students. We were told to find the second year at another college. Why? Didn't they trust us? Did they think ex-G.I.'s had unusually massive quotas of uncontrollable hormones bouncing around, waiting for release? Well, the girls found the boys and the boys

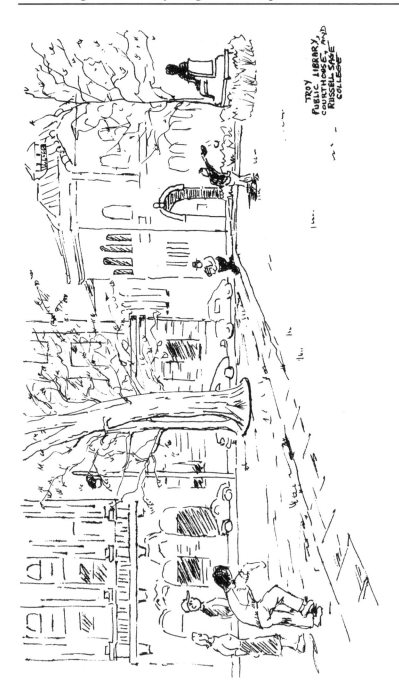

TROY PUBLIC LIBRARY, COURTHOUSE, AND RUSSELL SAGE COLLEGE

found the girls, regardless of any clear understandings.

Back then, we had pretty much the same beginning college courses as they have today: English, French, economics, psychology. I picked art as an elective.

The art teacher allowed me to go all over town and sketch. This was a teacher who bent the rules for the sake of the student. She got into hot water with the art department about letting me do this, but my teacher told them she had seen my drawings and liked my work and thought I was beyond beginning drawing. Still, it didn't sit well with the elderly chairperson who treasured and nurtured a rigid personality.

My teacher borrowed my drawings and showed the city sketches to her. Some were scenes of the downtown park with bums asleep on benches, people crossing city streets, scenes of the local bridge, and even a house of prostitution that flourished next to the railroad tracks.

Perhaps the pen and ink drawings were less than what was anticipated or less than what was formally required for the course. The meeting must have been confrontational because my teacher returned my pen and ink sketches with a frown, told me they were good, but suggested that perhaps I stay in class that week.

I'm sure I was the only art student in the history of the school who selected a house of prostitution as a study. I still wish I could have seen the look on the face of the prudish department head when she was told what the building represented. But my kindly, talented art teacher left at the end of the year and didn't return. A sad loss for the school.

When the second semester had finished at Russell Sage College, I worked in the local coal yard bagging and delivering coal. Coal was priced much cheaper in the summer and many customers took advantage of this.

Delivering was not easy because of the narrow, winding stairs in many of the homes. All too often, the fifty-pound bag that was hoisted on the shoulder, had to be maneuvered up three stories of narrow stairs, scraping the walls along the way. Being over six feet tall was a problem and often I had to climb the stairs on bended knees because of the low ceilings.

I tried carrying the coal bag all different ways—under my arm, in front of me, and even tried backing up the stairs—but none of these ways worked well. The shoulder carry was best and it was one of the times I wished I was shorter.

I had the muscles but not the maneuverability, so I was slower. After a half dozen of these trips, the driver, who was about five feet tall and quick, felt sorry for me and talked to the boss and told him that I was too tall for the job. Luckily, they had a job in the coal yard, bagging up coal for delivery trucks and putting coal in paper bags for grocery store sales.

The coal yard offered twenty-five-pound and fifty-pound bags only. At Uncle Dick's store, I made up any size bag of coal that the customer wanted, so bagging just two sizes was easier.

The anthracite coal came by freight car and was

dumped directly from the outside into several large metal bins that were afterwards covered over the top with movable tin. Each bin had a small gate at the bottom that was lifted up to let the coal pour out to fill the thick, tough canvas delivery sacks or paper bags.

The bagging room in the coal yard was an enclosed, unheated room with a single, small light bulb. Actually, light didn't matter much, because the room turned so black after the fifth filling of a bag that you couldn't see what you were doing anyway.

You filled about twenty bags of coal at a time, judging the height of the fill by feel, then went outside to breathe, and waited until the black dust cleared. When you could see, you weighed the bags and tied the tops with string. The job paid a dollar an hour which was a lot of money in 1947, and I was more than glad to get the work.

That fall, mostly through the recommendations of Morey Paine, the Y.M.C.A. Boy's Club Director, I was accepted at Middlebury College in Middlebury, Vermont. I was excited. Now I would prove myself in a regular daytime college which offered a lot more selection in courses.

My introduction to Middlebury started with the professor of Greek and Latin who was my advisor. He began by solemnly explaining I hadn't put down physical education as a course and that was something the faculty strongly recommended. To an Army infantry soldier who walked everywhere with full pack and was made to do calisthenics continuously, this advice was not appreciated.

The professor had other suggestions that were so wide off the mark that I had to disagree with them all. When I left, he was angry that I hadn't accepted a single suggestion. He had spent his life in a sheltered cocoon, teaching Greek and Latin to respectful students, year after year. I thought him odd, as he thought about me, but all too soon, I found he reflected the attitude of all the teachers at the school.

First, I began a language course in German. The professor had written a text—a slim meconium-colored book—that was concise, limited in vocabulary, and deadly boring. The teaching method was promoted by Dr. H. who was chairman of the department and each summer he taught other teachers how to teach.

He was a tall, thin man with abrupt mannerisms and unsmiling features. He would stalk into the classroom, pause silently, and look around the room for dramatic effect.

"Herr Jones," he would begin, "tell us how you would say the following *auf deutsch:* 'Instead of his mother, he visits his aunt.'"

If the student faltered, he would ask him if he had read the chapter and direct the same question to another student. Sometimes before the student could answer, he would ask someone else. Often he paused unnecessarily between his questions, so that the suspense would build up. A special trick of his was to slowly drawl out a student's name and then wait about ten seconds before asking the question.

Each class period was exactly the same. He questioned, you answered. If you asked a question, he would show you the answer was already in his book. And then he would stare at you.

No one was able to convince the faculty, through teacher evaluations, that this method of teaching held little pleasure for the students. Dr. H. was a well-meaning man who was teaching the way he was taught. And, of course, *his* teachers were taught the same way by *their* teachers, and none of them seem to comprehend that the teaching method they were handing down had frozen in time and never thawed.

If you learned, fine; if you struggled and had problems, then the suspicion was that perhaps you weren't cut out for learning languages and should quit.

I shudder at the thought of how many students were put off enjoying foreign languages because of this heavy-handed method of learning. If you were to judge strictly by the results, after finishing Dr. H.'s course, students who went to Germany and tried to use their knowledge of the language to rent a room, buy groceries, or change money would find themselves floundering and inadequate.

Speaking of floundering and inadequate, as soon as I walked into the art department, I knew I was in trouble.

Realism was out; abstract art with emphasis on expressing your inner "feelings" was in. I chatted with a few art teachers who explained that my idols Norman

Rockwell and Rockwell Kent were *illustrators* and not artists. At least not *real* artists. It was as though they were telling me that Walt Disney was just a businessman and not really creative.

After the art course at Russell Sage where I was permitted to wander outside and draw from life, well, I saw what the students were being taught to do here and the results were sad. At least, it wasn't what I wanted. Discouraged, I was on my own.

Although I did some drawing, I gave up on taking a formal art course and concentrated on creative writing. I wrote story after story but couldn't please the teacher. He wouldn't give me anything above grade *C* and often even that was *C minus.*

I worked hard at trying to follow the guidelines with a good beginning, a developed middle, and a solid ending, using the best grammar I could. One story I handed in and thought was my best effort; it came back with a *D plus* and the admonition that I could do better.

What was so wrong with my writing? I sat through class after class during which the girls received *A's* while their papers were read as standards for the rest of us to follow. They beamed with pleasure at the praise.

One day, however, the professor did pick my paper to read aloud. I was really proud just like those beaming girls. But when he finished reading it to the class, he reminded everyone that my work was a good example of a poor example of writing! The paper was about guard duty in the Army.

"Not believable," criticized the professor (even though he himself had never been in *any* military service.)

After that, I began to hate all the girls in the class. No matter what they wrote, they received a high grade. A few were even told to send their work off for publication. The *girls* were good!

Today, scientists tell us women have a better developed Broca's area of the brain and not only can articulate better than men, but are naturally better at speech and languages. I wish they would have discovered the brain differences when I was in college. I wouldn't have felt so badly.

I had been writing for years, ever since I left the grocery store, and never heard a compliment. Now at the end of my second year of college, I was so discouraged that I began to wonder why I ever tried to write in the first place. After all, a professor should know if you had it or didn't have it. Maybe I should try something else? I couldn't do worse.

So I dropped all liberal arts courses at Middlebury, such as philosophy, history of the ancients, English literature, and signed up for strictly science courses. The pleasure and surprise were immediate. Attending science courses was like breathing fresh air while riding a sensible Arabian horse.

The contrast was certain. Where liberal arts was groping in the smog, trying to qualify invisible objects; science was a clear, sunny day offering definable objects that could be quantified. Liberal arts, for me, was like being put in the same horse halter class, one after another, and never earning even a seventh place ribbon. Switching to the sciences was like entering numerous horseback endurance riding competitions and being awarded prize after prize.

I was happily on my way and, except for foreign languages, I never willingly took another liberal arts course again. I found that liberal arts was not for me, especially when I switched my courses over to sciences where, for the first time, I was so much happier.

But then there were other things I had to deal with. Like rules, like campus rules. There were campus rules that gave demerits for walking on the grass, for not wearing underclassmen beanies, for skipping daily chapel at 10:00 A.M. and skipping Sunday evening chapel where you were required to sit in certain seats. They actually paid a student to take church attendance and report if you neglected to wear a jacket and tie.

Complying with these rules was no problem with respectable boys and girls who hadn't seen anything of the war. But how could a foot soldier explain to these ivory-tower professors that ex-G.I.'s didn't consider walking on the grass or not taking "phys ed" or not wearing a tie as major disciplinary problems? I couldn't. And those teachers who thought of themselves as disciplinarians began disliking those of us who rebelled.

Perhaps I fit in with the philosophy later expressed by a Georgetown basketball coach who once said: "I probably couldn't play for me. I wouldn't like my attitude."

Similarly, I found that ex-G.I.'s must have the wrong attitude for obeying campus rules.

I began to find Middlebury more and more stifling, began to do poorly, and began to compensate by spending more and more time on the ski hill. I'll always be grateful for Middlebury's ski area and kindling a lifelong appreciation for skiing. As for college itself, Middlebury was not the best choice of schools for someone like me.

8

In the Mountains

8

In the Mountains

TOWARDS THE END OF THE FIRST SEMESTER at Middlebury College, a notice was posted on the bulletin board that the Universities of Michigan and Maryland had joined together to offer a supervised, accredited, third year of college in Switzerland. A student could pick the French-speaking or the German-speaking area, but two years of college credits of a foreign language were necessary.

I wrote and was accepted with the stipulation that I finish the second year of German in summer school. By half-starving, I saved up a good deal of the $75 per month from the G.I. Bill to pay for it.

That summer I signed up to enter the new language school being starting at Colby College in Waterville, Maine, which was the home of Morey Paine, who I met earlier at the Y.M.C.A. It was another way that he had helped me and another way to see a different state. In a few weeks, I passed the second year of German and I was on my way to Switzerland.

The trip on the *Queen Mary* cost only $100 from New York City to France. From there, a train took us into Basel,

Switzerland, where we were welcomed by Professor Ebelke from Wayne University. He and his wife oversaw twenty-nine American students of which five were girls. He was a conscientious administrator and tried hard to be everything to everyone.

Switzerland was almost unreal. The food was excellent, the accommodations were clean, and the Swiss were friendly but wary—after all, tourists were there all the time.

I lived in a home on Mittlere Strasse. The landlady had two sons in their early twenties who were amusing, so much so, that I asked if I could take my breakfast and evening meals with them. She was pleased to receive the extra money, and my evenings were spent listening to their family problems being discussed in a Swiss German dialect. I occasionally volunteered some thoughts in their dialect, which always broke up any serious conversation, so I was a welcomed guest at the dinner table.

I was to learn that each city had its own dialect and that someone from Bern can recognize citizens from Zurich or Lucern or Basel by their speech and vice versa. The Basel dialect was more difficult than "high" German; it was quite musical, whereas spoken German could be guttural and harsh. When I found a Basel dialect dictionary, which they didn't know existed, and began reading from it, they were surprised and doubly amused.

The University of Basel owned a large cabin in Engelberg which had the jaw-breaking name *Zschokkehaus*. It was located in the mountains, and dur-

ing Christmas break, we skied and took lessons with a large mixed group.

The Swiss girls were delightful but, unfortunately, immensely practical. I was twenty-two, very vulnerable to their charms, and madly interested in a different girl every few weeks. It was still the age of innocence though—at least, with the girls I met and dated. Nothing much happened beyond holding hands, but a little bit of that and you were invited to her home to meet the family. Going to church with the family on Sunday was the next step. The road became quite narrow shortly after, so I always declined the trip to church on Sunday.

In May, the school bulletin board posted a note requesting applications for the job of counselor at a boy's camp which had been named the "International Ranger Camp." I applied and, based on my Y.M.C.A. experience, was accepted as camp director.

I talked a few others in our college group into being counselors, and we worked for six weeks in a camp in Zug and in Interlaken. There were 106 children, ranging

Basel University and
Petersplatz

KUNSTMUSEUM

in age from eight to eighteen, mostly from the Army personnel stationed in Germany. I set up the schedules just as I had learned in New York which covered crafts, swimming, boating, and the like. We used whatever talents a particular counselor had. There were six counselors—five male and one female. One was a musician, another a magician, and another a dance professional. I think the campers had a good time—they seemed to have wanted to return the next year.

I fell for a Swiss counselor, Susi S., who was a music major, and after camp was over, I visited her home. I thought things were going well until one day during lunch, she carefully explained she couldn't take me seriously because I had no prospects—which was true. My chief aims were to ski well, learn yodeling, sing silly songs in German and French, and play the guitar. And oh, yes, continue going to school somehow. I had to agree: the vagabond scholar was hardly husband material.

The wood carvings in Switzerland were extraordinarily beautiful. We were on school holiday and I expressed interest in the artistry. A Swiss friend, Heinrich

Vollenweider, knew someone in the wood carving village from his compulsory military days and wrote a letter of introduction. I went to the village of Brienz and met Mr. Maier who made his living as a woodcarver. He read the letter and looked through my sketch book.

So many artists are gracious and kind about sharing their knowledge, and Mr. Maier was cast in the same mold. He not only offered me a room in his home for a few days, but helped me make a few carvings. I expressed an interest in staying a month after school was finished and learning more. He listened quietly, smiled at my enthusiasm, and gently pointed out that the formal woodcarving school in the village took six years.

That fall, upon returning to the States, I switched from

Middlebury to the University of Colorado. Once you've been in the mountains, it's difficult to be anywhere else. The G. I. Bill still was paying for tuition and subsistence, and where I went to school didn't matter as long as it wasn't Middlebury, it was accredited, and it had mountains. I ended up in Boulder.

By the time graduation rolled around in Colorado, the registrar was most unhappy that I had not followed any academic program, so she did her best to block granting me a bachelor's degree. But I had so many credits. Instead of following a pattern, I had taken any course that I thought would be interesting. The school officials highly disapproved of my "window shopping" program, but reluctantly dusted off an old rule and graduated me with two majors and two minors: German and French; chemistry and biology.

Even though I caught all kinds of flack for wandering about in college courses and taking five and a half years before graduating, I would do it again the same way. Especially living in a foreign country.

Should all students learn a foreign language and spend a supervised year in their favorite foreign country? I don't know.

For me, I think I needed to learn how similar everyone was in the world. Being in a war makes you cynical when you realize how you were maneuvered to hate certain masses of people. But once you live or work with these very same people whom you were trained to hate, it's difficult to be an "ugly" American.

When you are aware of their culture and background, foreigners simply become *friends* with a different outlook who can be understood if only given the time to know them and who can be understood if you take the time to understand.

Take the time. So easy to say and so hard to do.

9
Guilt and
Former Chums

Chums

9
Guilt and Former Chums

Y OU MAKE SO MANY FRIENDS wherever you go. Often you're together because of a common goal, and when that goal is reached, you move on to the next phase of your life. Moving on has been difficult for me. It's like throwing away a comfortable pair of shoes or an old jacket.

For years, I felt guilty about not keeping in contact with the friends I had made over the years. Often we sweated through all kinds of troubles, knew intimate details of each other's lives, and took for granted that we would forever help each other anytime we could.

There were always the lack of money, loves that were won and lost, school grades that came out lower than expectations, promises kept and unkept—all of which brought us closer together. Then the period of time was over, and we lost track of each other. Friendships, especially if distances were involved, were more easily neglected or dropped, and the golden times were never to be recaptured.

The guilt was deserved, I felt, because something was

lacking in me, that I was, no, must be, a superficial person for not being more attentive and taking the time to shore up the timbers of friendship. If only I had written or phoned. I alibied that medicine was a jealous mistress and demanded an enormous amount of time just to keep current in the field. Just the same, I blamed myself for letting the time lapse, although the few times that I tried to take up where we left off as friends, were not to be.

It didn't take much more than one of us acquiring a wife and the other still remaining single. Or one of us still worried about school exams and the other settled in business.

"Would you like to buy some insurance?" sort of dampens a beginning conversation, especially if it occurs during the first few minutes of a chat. A little time more in the visit, and we both realize our priorities and interests had changed considerably. And we're both embarrassed for each other.

Jim M. was a typical college chum. He decided, early on, to become a German language teacher. We were together during the third year of college in Switzerland. When he wrote a few years later, the tone of his letters had begun to change—less humor and more about working up the academic ladder. His viewpoint about students was less charitable, and more a lament about how poorly trained the average high school graduate was in the English language and how he had to teach basic English grammar along with German.

Was this coming from the hippie who prided himself

on never getting a haircut? The hippie who did im-promptu tap dances in the streets, sang loudly wherever he went, and went out of his way to joyfully break every college rule he could find?

About twenty years after the change in tone of his letters, I had a job of inspecting a hospital laboratory for the College of Pathologists in the vicinity where he and his wife lived. During dinner in their home, I began talk-ing about Jim's impressive *joie de vivre* and the good times we had in college. I should have been warned when his Scandinavian-born wife and two children looked startled.

Those were happy, carefree college days I said and began to blithely describe our escapades: how we "snuck in" wine at the yearly Basal University Ball and got caught; how we borrowed bicycles from two wealthier students, promising to use them only for a few hours and went clear across Switzerland to St. Gallen on them; how we chased girls during a ski vacation; how Jim insisted on making up long, involved, shaggy dog tales and telling them in the German language to anyone he could cap-ture; how Jim insisted on composing the official Basal Universitaet school song as soon as he found they didn't have one—which infuriated the Swiss students that an American had to come over and teach them about the lack of school spirit; how Jim really messed up—

His foreign-born wife interrupted and corrected me sharply. "James would never do such things. What's more, I've never seen James without a necktie and a white shirt, or when he was not perfectly groomed. Why on earth would he be silly enough to make a fool of himself danc-ing in the streets? You are obviously making this all up!"

I tried to soften her barrage and tell her that at the time we *all* wanted to be like Gene Kelly who danced in the movie *Singing in the Rain*, and that Jim's footwork was the best attempt I had ever seen.

She wasn't listening. "What would people think?" she continued. "What if this irrational behavior was reported to the university officials? Especially to faculty members in the language department, some of whom dislike him anyway?"

She thought for a moment and was now glaring, "What's more, it isn't very nice of you to make up such awful stories that could only get James into trouble."

We both looked at Jim and we both wanted confirma-tion of sorts. I wanted Jim to regale us with a few of the funny stories and remind me of things we did that I had forgotten. His wife, on the other hand, was looking at him in a strange manner, as if he was someone she didn't really know.

Finally, after a long silence, Jim sighed and said, "I don't know why you're making up those stories, Harry. I wish I could go along with it. It sounds like fun, but it sure isn't anything that I remember doing."

"See!" his wife smiled triumphantly. "I knew James couldn't do such foolish things. You got him mixed up with someone else."

I felt so sad. It was a heavy sadness.

I remembered a book I purchased in Switzerland, foolishly squandering the few francs I had to spend to buy it instead of lunch, only because I was intrigued with the title *Nie Kehrst Du Wieder, Goldene Zeit* [Never Will You Return, Golden Times]. I must have been fighting then, against the day when we were to leave and get on with our lives. Somehow I had a premonition that everything we were doing was going to be packed up in time and memory, and never recur. Never to return.

Now here it was . . . actually happening!

The hippie who I enjoyed laughing with and pulling pranks with, that delightful, humorous pal who rebelled against all stifling restrictions, was now a serious, immaculately groomed, ultraconservative. I was looking at someone I lost.

Jim was no longer Jim but *Doctor James*, and I was sitting opposite a stranger who was very much aware of his professorship, his peers, and his distinguished faculty responsibilities at the university, which he didn't want to jeopardize by saying or doing anything that could be criticized, even from the past.

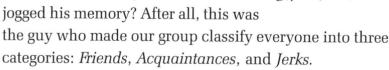

DR. JAMES

How did he manage to completely repress everything? Should I have jogged his memory? After all, this was the guy who made our group classify everyone into three categories: *Friends*, *Acquaintances*, and *Jerks*.

Would he had remembered and said what he always

said, "This categorization is one of my best accomplish-ments"? Would he had remembered interrupting conversations about someone and asking, "Which is he, *F*, *A*, or *J*?" then afterwards laughing and laughing at our stumbling attempts to categorize the person?

I didn't try.

And we never visited or wrote to each other again.

10

Medical School and Dr. Whipple

Dr. George H. Whipple
DEAN

10
Medical
School and
Dr. Whipple

WHAT MAKES A PERSON SELECT MEDICINE for his life's work?

Remember it was right after World War II, and everyone was seeking answers to a lot of questions. Introspection was the order of the times, and there were many popular publications about the meaning of life. Like others, I read everything I could.

Will Durant and his wife were extraordinarily capable of explaining the views of various philosophers to ordinary people like myself. One special favorite of mine remains their book entitled *The Story of Philosophy*. Of course, the viewpoints are often contradictory and depend so much upon the personality of the philosopher.

After reading and trying to understand so many different ideas, I felt a special kinship with the musician/medical doctor Albert Schweitzer and his term "reverence for life." Living things mattered the most—they were what lasted and lasted. Material things were temporary. His thoughts were very instrumental in making up my mind to become a medical doctor.

When school at Boulder finished, in December, 1951, I became a member of the regular ski patrol at Winter Park, Colorado. When the ski area closed, I went to see a surgeon, Dr. E. Guy Ceriani, in Kremmling, which was a short distance west.

I knew he was busy, being the only doctor in the town, and I knew he was famous. In 1948, *Life* magazine had placed him on their front cover, showing him drinking a cup of coffee, before amputating a gangrenous leg.

I didn't know any physicians. All my school contacts had been with doctors who had purely academic backgrounds. What was the reality of medical practice? Would blood make me cringe? Would sick people bother me? Would Dr. Ceriani help me answer these questions?

DR.
CERIANI.

I proposed to ask if I could follow him around for a week and pay back his time by working in the hospital. Expecting to be rebuffed, I still took a bus to Kremmling, hoping to meet this physician.

Dr. Ceriani was not only gracious about letting me follow him around, but he let me live in the basement of the hospital. I paid him back by cleaning out a few old storerooms, but that wasn't much for what I was getting in return.

I discovered I liked everything about the hospital and medical practice. I watched Dr. Ceriani stop acute bleeding, treat arthritis, check anemia, diagnose illnesses, and perform tonsillectomies. It was with great relief I found that gushing blood and gore didn't bother me.

Thanks to a humble, caring, thoughtful, and dedicated doctor like Dr. Ceriani, after that week, I was sure of what I wanted to do in life.

From there, I visited different schools in the East, beginning with Johns Hopkins, but the registrars were cold and discouraging. So much for first choices.

Should I go back to Colorado? No. Colorado made it clear they wanted only Colorado residents in their graduate schools.

Then what was wrong with *my* home state where I was considered a New York resident? I figured it was worth a try.

So I found a New York State Competitive Scholarship, applied, took the exam, and qualified. Armed with a scholarship, I began visiting medical schools in New York, but hit one stone wall after another. Still on the bus, almost as a lark, I decided to check with Rochester Medical School.

I walked into the office and asked to see the dean. Since registrars had a certain discouraging sameness to them, I knew this was a ridiculous request. But why not? The worst that could happen would be to get tossed out.

The secretary surprised me by smiling and calling Dean Whipple out of his research lab. I introduced myself and he ushered me into his office.

What a shock! The small, sparse room contained only one old desk and two older chairs. The walls were not just poorly decorated; they were not decorated at all! Unpainted, gray, mason brick enclosed the room. It looked like the inside of a poor auto garage.

The room was so different from the norm; it was understated elegance. The battered desk and old chairs spoke volumes about the inhabitant. By not seeking to impress, Dr. Whipple became all the more impressive.

He didn't need a fancy desk, wall-to-wall carpeting, paintings or honors and academic degrees glaring at you from the walls, although he had every right to brag about his awards, to show them off, even spotlight them if he wished. But he didn't. After all, Dr. Whipple was not only dean, pathologist, founder of Rochester Medical School, but also a Nobel Prize winner.

We talked and talked, and liked each other immediately. Sadly, he explained that I was old at twenty-six to begin medical school; they wanted younger students. Just the same, he didn't want to discourage me and had me meet some professors. Dr. Mason, head of the Anatomy Department, offered me a position that would lead to an instructorship in human anatomy. Since I had had several courses in embryology and comparative anatomy, it would fit in well. I accepted on the spot.

Dean Whipple felt my age was against me, and if that wasn't enough, I entered that fall as the only married student in the class. Had he known, I'm sure he would have had second thoughts about encouraging me to continue studies at all. Today, of course, older students and married students are perfectly acceptable, but in 1952, the medical schools felt older students were less able to learn and that marriage was a disabling distraction from the necessary long hours of study.

Anatomy class began on a bad note. The associate professor in charge of anatomy was a Ph.D. He was mean-spirited and did many unkind things. Once, when he was asked a simple question, he spun around, and called all the freshman medical students into a different room. He wrote "20:1" on the blackboard and glared at us.

He scowled, "Anyone want to guess what that means?"

A few amusing remarks came back, and he waited until they were finished. He glowered, then spit out the words, "Just a

reminder. There are twenty applicants for each of your places here. You're here to *answer* questions, not *ask* them! Do I make myself clear?"

The entire room became silent at such a naked threat. He dismissed us and told us to return to the dissecting rooms. As time went on, we found he disliked medical students, felt threatened by them, and compensated by bullying vulnerable freshmen students. I realized I would not be able to work under him in his department and would have to switch majors or apply elsewhere. Yet, the course work seemed to be going well.

But during the third week of the anatomy course, a very embarrassed Dr. Mason approached me outside.

"We like our students to wear neckties," he said. Thinking a moment longer, he added, ". . . and *white* shirts."

I couldn't help wonder why I was being singled out to dress up for dissecting a grubby, smelly corpse. The next day, I looked around at the men in the anatomy class. Sure enough, every male student wore a white shirt and necktie while dissecting their opened cadavers. They must have *always* worn white shirts and neckties, and I simply missed noting it. The five girls in class were also dressed up with their hair perfect and lipstick applied. I stuck out like a sore thumb.

The relaxed dress code of Colorado did not apply here. I owned only two shirts and hated soiling them both with the fatty substance from cadavers and wrecking them with overpowering formalin fumes. Still, a dress code was a dress code.

The Physiology Department seemed to be filled with unusual researchers. One professor gathered up the excess dog hair that we had cut off while we were working on our animals, went into his private lab, and after a short time, came out with a beaker filled with thin, black syrup.

With great delight, he explained that he had transformed the dog hair into nutritious protein.

He took a large spoon and tried to get students to taste it. No one would, even though he himself sampled spoonful after spoonful. I still remember the sad look on his face. "It's excellent protein!" he kept exclaiming. "You must at least try it!" He was *so* proud of his achievement and *so* disappointed in us.

The head of that same department looked like General Omar Bradley. He was only content when he could talk about physiology and was delighted to explain that the human body was a miracle of achievement. How we speak, the movement of the arms and legs, swallowing food, and on and on with each bodily miracle. He was thrilled to go into detail about the nerves, muscles, blood supply, or whatever was necessary for every bodily function. It was a nonstop monologue, punctuated with "Tell me, how would you go about proving . . . ? " One topic led to another which led to another, yet another, and another, forever more.

We thought we were safe from his mania when we went to his home for a party. His wife had rescued too many people who invariably became zombies and developed glazed eyes while talking to her husband. In desperation, since scolding did nothing, she made him hold a rubber ball and squeeze it every time he felt the urge to talk about physiology.

"Tell me about yourself," he'd start. "Where are you from?" After responding, someone asked a return question. Immediately, the professor launched into his favorite phrase, "How would you go about proving . . . ?" only to have his wife appear.

With a beatific smile on his face, he would stop talking in mid-sentence, reach into his pocket, bring out the rubber ball, and begin squeezing it. He had obeyed the commandment, but his face reflected the same sadness as his colleague who made the protein from the excess dog hair.

One of the most inspiring teachers I ever met was Dean Whipple, a pathologist. The course he taught in general pathology was overwhelming in breath of content: the textbook alone was four-and-a-half inches thick. But he wanted us to keep studying, keep learning, be open-minded, and not get discouraged. On more than one occasion, he would emphasize the privilege of practicing medicine.

He asked students questions that were important to the care of a patient. "What is a normal white blood count?" he would ask.

The answer would lead to related questions: "What types of cells are they?" "What are the names and functions of the different white blood cells?" "How would you go about proving that these are actually the functions of those particular cells?"

No one was graded on the answers, but we tried to do our best. He would always give guided hints and always praise students afterwards on how well they did, even though he put the words in their mouth.

You could tell he liked his students by the way he was pulling for them when they stumbled for the answers. It was more the Socratic method without the penetrating dagger or wit. His calm demeanor and quickness to praise anyone's efforts endeared him to us, the lowly beginning medical students, because all too often we were told by others, "You're here to answer questions, Mister, not ask them!"

What Dr. Whipple taught best, without even knowing it, was dignity. Quietly, but persistently, he would project a special dignity.

As you sat there and watched and listened to him, you felt this quality of respect applied to *everyone*—not just to our faculty or to our patients or to each other, but to everyone. Cynicism, distrust, and clever witticisms were for others to exercise. He taught the dignity of being a teacher and his choice of teaching happened to be medicine.

That's why so many of us, who were fortunate enough to be taught by him, became pathologists. It was that special dignity he radiated and communicated. It was as though he expected great things of us, like reaching for the stars and actually touching them.

So I suppose, when many of us did become pathologists, it was sort of a clumsy way of thanking him and saying, "I'm going to try. I may not make it, but I'll try my best to measure up."

Unfortunately, when Dean Whipple retired from his position, a new person came in who was a graduate of

Harvard. The change was shattering. Things began to be done the *right* way, which we suspected was the way of his alma mater.

He commandeered a large oversized office near the front of the hospital; had thick, bright red carpeting installed; decorated the walls with prints and medical awards; and sat behind a large, expensive desk. A separate attached office held two secretaries. The hospital/school affiliation was renamed a "Medical Center" and everything began to be discussed in terms of numbers.

In his initial talks to us, the new person explained the importance of percentages and compared Rochester to the various percentages achieved in other medical schools. Everything was categorized and there were percentages for everything, such as the grade averages of entering students, grade averages of graduates compared to their grade averages in undergraduate school, percentages of graduates that finished, percentages that became specialists, percentages of different categories of specialists, *etcetera ad nauseum.*

Our Dean Whipple, a warm, friendly, humble human who took a personal interest in every student's problems, was replaced by a cold, efficient, terribly self-impressed physician-accountant from an Ivy League college.

All year, I had an unsettled feeling. I wasn't certain how I was doing because grades were not given out. I was used to being one of the bright ones in the class; but now, everyone was not only bright, but *very* bright. Indeed, two of our class members took only two years to finish four years of college while I had delighted in taking five and a half years.

The stated reason by the faculty for not giving out grades was so we wouldn't be competitive with each other. But all too often, the lectures were completely different from the quizzes. Why didn't the class complain?

Well, to find out, no one complained because everyone had the old exams. Everyone, that is, except me. And the teachers hadn't changed anything in those exams year after year. Since there was no correlation of the lectures with the exams, if you didn't have a copy of the old exams, you were dead.

I was dead.

A good friend and fellow student was Bob M. He ate with us, played games with us, and when his girl visited, she stayed with us. We couldn't have been closer as friends.

When I discovered it was necessary to have the old exams, I became suspicious of Bob doing so well and got him to confess, under some duress, that he had copies of all the old exams. *All* of them!

"You didn't show me any?" I reprimanded, feeling betrayed. "Why not? I'm your best friend."

"You'd get a good grade and raise the curve," he said. "I have to think of myself first."

11

Marquette and Joe

JOE

11

Marquette and Joe

THINKING OF MYSELF FIRST, I moved back to Milwaukee, entered Marquette Graduate School, and then Marquette Medical School. The atmosphere was completely different from Rochester. The students liked one another and tried to help each other. No one spouted percentages. What's more, the instructors liked the students, and the students liked the instructors. In this climate, I began to blossom, did well in everything that I attempted, and even had time to publish a half dozen research papers.

The most exciting time was the first day on the medical wards at the Milwaukee County Hospital. We were all so proud and self-conscious of our new stethoscopes, hammers, and notebooks.

I was assigned to Dr. Abboud, an internist from Egypt, who was in his third year of specialty training and spoke broken English. His first question, after I introduced myself, was, "What do you know about 'essential' hypertension?"

I explained what we had been taught and added that the word "essential" actually meant "unknown cause."

"Unknown cause?" he smiled cryptically. "Hmm . . . this ward has twenty patients with hypertension. I want you to take a history from each of them. As soon as you find certain similarities in their histories, you can stop and come back. We'll talk about it."

Puzzled, I did as I was assigned. After interviewing the sixth patient, I decided they had something definitely in common and went back to Dr. Abboud.

"So?" he queried.

"Anger," I said. "They're angry at everything. On the outside they appear relaxed and full of good humor, but it doesn't take much to stir up deep feelings of antagonism. All of them have been married several times, one for six times. All of them have had over a dozen jobs in a short time. They're all smoldering volcanoes."

"Good!" Dr. Abboud said. "You did well. Now, perhaps you will rethink 'essential' hypertension and its causes."

I spoke slowly. "They didn't mention this in lectures."

"No. That's why you're here, on the wards, where you *really* learn about patients. Now, what medicines would you prescribe for these particular hypertensives?"

I admitted, "I already read the charts. Different doctors have prescribed different medications."

"Yes . . . but what would *you* prescribe, knowing what you know?"

I thought for a moment. "Probably temporary medication with more of a thrust to changing their mental attitudes."

Thoughtfully, he said, ". . . Yes . . . changing their mental attitudes *would* change their blood pressures and their health."

I was elated. It was my first day on the medical wards and already I had concluded something that was not only important, but was also something new to ponder. In this day and age, however, this conclusion is well accepted.

After a week on the wards, I noticed that when a patient wasn't getting better, in spite of extensive medication and treatment, the medical residents would have a group discussion.

"Let's run this by Joe and see what he thinks."

Discussion group after discussion group ended up the same way. It seemed every difficult problem patient eventually needed Joe's input.

I had to meet Joe.

Joe turned out to be a normal-sized person, a bit on the wiry side physically, who presented a somewhat scholarly, preoccupied air. His bearing was pleasant enough, but as you watched him, you were struck by his lack of excessive or wasted movements. His physical examination routine was exact and thorough, and his diagnoses were clearly stated without face-saving double talk.

Joe interpreted an illness differently. He treated the patient and not the disease; he understood the expression of the disease in each particular patient. Something we're told to do, but often forget.

I introduced myself and shamelessly followed him

everywhere he went. I copied down everything Joe said to other resident doctors and what he ordered on patients. Every night I went over and over his comments, and his favorite medications. Each difficult case he solved, I wrote down in detail and committed them to memory. Slowly, by trying to match his thought patterns and studying his approach to patients, I became adept.

I talked and walked like Joe. My stethoscope and pens were carried in the same pockets as Joe carried them in his pockets. Any new word or medical article he mentioned, I wrote down to learn or read. It took long hours on the wards, far more than required; volumes of careful notes from researching the illnesses; and a cheerful willingness to perform any task for anyone at any hour.

Soon, other resident doctors, with several years of training ahead of me, observed my diligence and started identifying me with Joe. They had to. Where Joe was, I was.

They began asking me to examine their patients and write any orders I thought necessary. They asked me questions about unusual diseases, suggested patients I should seek out and examine to further my knowledge. The moment I came on the wards, they would stop me.

"Go down to the next ward . . . splinter hemorrhages under the fingernails—septicemia."

"Melanoma case with satellitosis . . . interested?"

"Cushing's Syndrome in Ward Three."

"Patient with classic myxedema, third bed, Ward Five."

How can I explain what a heady experience it was,

wanting desperately to excel in a chosen field and to be asked, as a beginning junior medical student, to check out problem patients and actually write orders on the charts for improving their therapy? Naturally, I copied everything I said and did for Joe to critique immediately afterwards. I well knew one mistake would completely sear my credibility.

As a medical student, I called the other resident doctors "doctor" but this resident doctor I called "Joe." It was mainly because Joe was comfortable to be around, he talked ordinary English, and he told us to call him by his first name. It made sense to him, and I think that was why he was the finest doctor in the hospital: he used common sense.

I remember Joe explaining a patient's options to another resident doctor. He ended enumerating them with these words, ". . . and there's the final option of doing nothing."

Doing *nothing*? Clearly, that hadn't occurred to the other doctor. In this case, Joe strongly hinted that doing nothing was the best option, because time was going to heal this patient better than additional medications.

Also, Joe used the laboratory tests selectively. Most beginning resident doctors ordered a barrage of lab tests, so they couldn't be criticized in the weekly conferences for overlooking something.

When Joe was asked why he hadn't ordered a test, he replied, with a grin, "Didn't need it. Why bother?"

If the questioner persisted and said the patient should

have the test for a baseline, Joe would smile and not dignify the questioner with a reply. Joe didn't hassle anyone and didn't allow himself to be hassled.

When some new, esoteric treatment was brought up at the conferences, and Joe was asked his opinion, he would sometimes reply, "Can we wait and see? What we have now is working just fine."

Down the line, all too often, the new treatment didn't work at all as promised, like some of the "new" antibiotics that were given in improper dosages, resulting in irreversible damage to the patient. Somehow Joe had a gut feeling to "wait and see."

When huge efforts were being expended to keep a very terminal cancer patient alive who was not enjoying a moment of living, Joe would quietly suggest the patient might be better off without so many needles, fluids, and painful operations. It was a shocking, callous thing to say at the time, and as it still is today, when doctors and nurses are caught up in prolonging life, sparing no expense and nothing in the medical armamentarium. However, after the idea was presented, logic and common sense took over and dictated. Indeed, less heroic measures were indicated in the case.

If I were given a choice of attributes to select as my own, not from a physician's point of view but of a human being, it would be how Joe used common sense. Common sense, as they say, is truly uncommon. If you have it, you are a very fortunate person.

My fortune was to discover someone like Joe who allowed me to follow him around like a leech; prolong his workday for many more hours by answering my questions; and put up with my mimicking his every thought, every speech pattern, and every mannerism. I did try to learn everything from Joe—especially his common sense, which was an integral part of his craftsmanship.

But try as I would, I never quite made it. One really *knows*, you know. It was the one thing he couldn't teach me.

But I never stopped trying, never stopped working, and always hoped that someday, somehow, the work I did would touch his level of craftsmanship.

12

Internship on the wards

Internship

12

Internship on the Wards

Think how terribly exciting it is to enter a hospital ward and know you can do something worthwhile to make a sick person better.

It's a heartwarming experience to look at patients, listen to their ailments, make an educated guess—then follow it up with confirming tests. In order to make the diagnosis, the challenge is to *look* and *listen* more than examine. It's more than just a matter of training and more apt to be called the "art" of medicine.

It's using good sense in many ways such as not hurrying patients and letting them tell their story their own way; not interrupting; not allowing moral judgment to enter into the relationship; in other words, trying to be a genuine friend—a friend who has spent time acquiring the necessary knowledge to be helpful—to a sick person.

My first assignment was to the charity ward at St. Elizabeth Hospital in Youngstown, Ohio. Lung diseases were common because the steel mills spewed forth many pollutants into the air from their huge stacks. Every morning, the streets were covered with a fine layer of brown-red dust which blew all over. The interior of every home had a similar fine layer of dust. So, when I canvassed the ward for various ailments, I found, naturally enough, respiratory problems were most common.

The ward also had its share of diabetics, severe cardiacs, and victims of stroke. The saddest were a few patients who were terminal. Outwardly, they acted as though they weren't aware of it and occasionally asked why they didn't improve, but hardly listened to any answers about their problem illness.

Now, for the first time, I had my own patients and would be able to diagnose, treat, and watch how they improve.

My first patient on the ward was an elderly woman who had been in the hospital for three months. She had a history of intermittent diarrhea and constipation. We had been taught that such a history, especially in the elderly, requires a work-up for intestinal cancer. I put on a glove and palpated the rectum. Sure enough, there was an encircling cancer present. The pathologist confirmed it from a biopsy. Unfortunately, the cancer had invaded significantly.

This was a humbling initiation to realize that I wouldn't be very helpful to some patients—no matter what. Then all too soon, I was to be humbled again, only a little more drastically.

It happened when a nursing student asked if I was the new intern on the ward, and I replied that I was. She handed me a tray containing a syringe filled with fluid and told me an attending physician wanted the medication given intravenously to an elderly man.

I asked what medication was in the syringe and the answer was that it was the usual digitalis medication he received regularly. I injected the solution.

Moments later, the charge nurse came out and asked how much of the syringe I had injected. The patient was to have had only half the medicine!

So much for giving an unknown quantity of "regular" medicine to an unknown patient. I filled out and signed an Incident Report on myself and received a well-deserved dressing down from the attending surgeon, the residents, the educational advisor Dr. Ginder, and other interns.

I sat with the patient for hours whenever I could—more in embarrassment than concern that he would die. The patient recovered without incident, although his pulse rate slowed down to the 50's for a few days.

Never again in my practice would I accept a filled syringe from anyone.

Many times later, nurses asked me why I didn't trust them when I refused to inject syringe-filled medications that I was given. I told them one bad experience was enough, and that I always read the label and filled the syringe myself.

One nurse, who was a personal friend, became angry when I refused her proffered syringe. After my brief explanation, she thought about it and said, "You're the doctor I want to take care of me when I'm sick." She went and got the medicine container for me and a clean, sterile, empty syringe.

If I felt any satisfaction of being in complete charge of the ward, another incident occurred in the main ward that unsettled me, but it made me forever careful to follow exact procedures.

I was on my way to a meeting when the nurse from blood service asked me to start a pint of blood on a patient. I checked the cross-match slip, found the numbers matched, and entered the room.

I asked the patient if her name was Mrs. Casandra Turner. She said she was. I said her doctor wanted her to have a pint of blood. She said fine and lay down on the bed.

I started the beginning saline in the tube into her arm, and once I saw it was flowing well, I began the blood to follow the saline line. Then I checked her arm band. It read "Martha Smith."

Aghast, I said, "You told me your name was Mrs. Casandra Turner!"

She looked at me quite pleasantly and said, "If you want me to be Casandra Turner, it's okay with me."

I could only scold myself. Wrist bands are placed on the patient's wrist for a reason. No procedure is to take place without first reading the name and comparing it with the order. It's something that had been drilled into us.

Luckily, the blood hadn't reached the entrance to the blood vessel, but once again I had to make out an Incident Report on myself. Would I ever learn?

The charity ward receives the great unwashed and homeless. I was only on the ward for a few days when the police brought in a patient covered with maggots. The nurses were nauseated at the sight of hundreds of live maggots crawling out of the patient's ears, mouth, and nose—in fact, out of every opening in the body.

The mass was writhing, wriggling, and dropping on the floor, escaping under the bed and table. An occasional fly would buzz us. The nurses, with good reason, kept gagging and leaving after a few minutes. They apologized for not having him ready for a physical examination.

I took the wash basins and cleaned up the patient. It took more than an hour. The nurses kept coming in, gagging, apologizing, and thanking me for doing their work.

I found I didn't mind—it was a job that had to be done. I didn't tell them that it was a lot easier than other jobs I had, such as an infantry soldier sloughing through mud, or like bagging coal in the dark and not being able to breathe, or balancing a wheelbarrow of wet cement up a loose plank knowing you'd be fired if you spilled it, or working in a flour mill loading flour bags into freight cars as fast as you could. Compared to those jobs, cleaning hundreds of writhing, wriggling maggots was child's play.

But the nurses didn't quite see it that way. Afterwards, to show their respect and gratitude, they detailed a nurse to follow me every time I made my rounds so I didn't have to write down orders on patients. When I left the ward, the staff baked a large chocolate cake with the words "Our Hero!" on it.

However, I found that being friendly with the nurses was not always best for the patient. For example, a patient was in a coma, tossing and turning in her bed with discomfort. I examined her and decided that she had a full urinary bladder, so I requested catheterization "stat" which means "right away."

Fifteen minutes later when I came back, the patient was still in agony. This shouldn't be. Apparently, my diagnosis was wrong.

I went to the nurses' station and said I had made a wrong diagnosis and was mistaken—my patient was still uncomfortable after being relieved. I would have to do some tests immediately and find the problem.

The nurses looked embarrassed and said they hadn't performed the catheterization.

"Why not?" I asked.

Well, it seemed Doctor X, who was known for his foul temper, came in right after I gave my order and left a lot of orders on his patients. Since they were afraid of him and his anger, they took care of his patients right away. I was considered a "nice" doctor and they knew I would be understanding about their workload.

I took the rubber tube and catheterized the patient myself. She immediately stopped her moaning and restless rolling. It was such a tremendous relief to see her relax. I was worried I had missed something very serious such as a brain injury, and had delayed doing something about it.

When I had time to reflect about this incident, it made me realize that I wasn't doing my patients any favors by being perceived as "a nice guy." If the foul-tempered doctors received quick and better service for their patients, then to be fair to my patients, the least I should do was to become less amiable. So I became less friendly with the nursing staff and made sure each order I gave was followed in a reasonable time. When it wasn't, I quietly but firmly conveyed my displeasure.

Again, it was another important learning experience during internship which taught the new doctor how to deal not only with patients, but also with his own professional groups.

13
E. R.

"HOW MANY BOMBINGS have you had so far in Youngstown?" A question often asked.

The Mafia was beginning to muscle in; gambling, prostitution, and corruption flourished; and I was there in 1959 on my next assignment in the emergency room (E. R.).

During the first week, an attractive blonde lady came into E. R. to visit her boyfriend who had been warned off from dating her. She said she had broken up with a Mafia hoodlum and preferred this man—who got beaten up for continuing to date her.

The beating didn't stop his efforts so, a few nights later, he was brought back in, tightly holding his abdomen to keep his intestines from spilling out. It seemed that he had turned the ignition key and his car exploded.

You see, the most common method of reprisal for the Organization was to attach a bomb to the ignition switch of an auto. Two mechanics made a good living, full-time, checking out automobiles for bombs and removing them. But they missed this one or were never called.

I was proud of how I handled the victim: lab tests, cross-matching blood, shock blocks, and intravenous fluids going in both arms and legs.

So I was surprised to get a call from an irate surgical resident, asking me, "How could you be so dumb? " (Everything a new doctor does is the "greatest" or the "dumbest." There seems to be no in-between.) "Think about what you did that was stupid!"

I listed everything out loud and gave up.

I did the unthinkable. I ordered X-rays on the patient and sent him to the X-ray department with only an X-ray technician in attendance. At that time of night, no one would have been there if the patient had a sudden hemorrhage or had gone into shock. I should have been there, just in case. Another lesson learned early in my internship.

The blonde? She came in with a beautiful, full-length fur coat, a gift from the hoodlum, and said they were on their way to Miami.

As for other bombings, there were the usual incidents at businesses who didn't pay or who were slow in paying the recommended amount of "insurance" money.

For example, when some doctors from St. E.'s were eating dinner in a restaurant and a nearby wall exploded, all the waiters calmly ushered everyone into another dining room, and began repairing the large hole and piling up the bricks in neat rows.

When the police came, the waiters acted innocently. No, they never heard a loud noise. The hole in the wall with the plywood over it? Perhaps there was some sort of gas line explosion early that afternoon—nothing to do with them. They were going to check with the gas company the next day. The police left disgusted.

Even the shootings by the Organization were clear in their intent. When a bondsman got out of his car in the driveway of his home, the sound of a shotgun blast, that was very close by, would cause him to drop to the ground. The assailants drove their car leisurely through the bondsman's circular driveway and shot shell after shell towards the bondsman, carefully missing him. Obviously, a message.

These "messages" were never reported by the victims. Usually a neighbor or a passerby reported it, and the victims denied anything happened. In this case, the gunshots were so loud in the residential area, the gunmen so leisurely in their driving, that there were plenty of witnesses. The newspaper sent out a reporter, but the bondsman couldn't recall seeing or hearing anything out of the ordinary. He was quoted as saying, "If I heard anything, then I forgot it, because I thought it was a car backfiring."

Youngstown made no pretense about their Organization. The newspaper, *Youngstown Vindicator*, almost daily, named individuals, places, and illegal events—with no reaction from the law enforcement officials. It almost seemed as though the Organization was pleased to be recognized for their achievements in print.

In E. R., an elderly Italian gentleman entered with a

blood pressure problem. I phoned his doctor for orders and was told to give his patient an intravenous dose of reserpine. His six sons were gathered around the hospital bed—two in the uniforms of firemen, one in the uniform of a policeman.

The father asked me where I was from. When I said Troy, New York, his eyes glinted with caution. He began to talk Italian to me. I shook my head and said I was Armenian. That didn't quiet his anxiety. He spoke carefully in Italian to his sons.

When the nurse handed me the vial of reserpine she had opened, I started to fill up the syringe. The father spoke again. One of the sons asked to see the vial. They solemnly passed it around to each other, carefully reading the label and asking me questions about it. I replied that their father had very high blood pressure and that this would lower it, but there would be an initial, awful feeling with it that would pass in fifteen or twenty seconds.

The father shook his head and spoke. One of the sons asked who had opened the vial. I said the nurse did. They wanted a fresh unopened vial. We threw away the opened one, and the nurse brought an unopened vial which they again passed around and read the label. Then they took the vial and called their doctor. When it was confirmed, the son handed back the vial to me and I filled the syringe.

"Remember," I said, "your father will feel poorly for a very short time."

I injected the fluid. After a few seconds, the father turned pale and angry. Half raising himself on one elbow, he pointed to me and shouted to his sons, "Get him, boys! He's killed me!"

All six sons turned to me and I quickly said, as relaxed as I could appear, "Remember what I said about his not feeling good for a little while?"

"That's fine, Doc," said one of the sons. "Just the same, don't plan on going anywhere right away."

Confident, but pressured with all those suspicious eyes, I stood for awhile and finally sat down on a chair next to the bed. When their father began to feel better, I took his blood pressure and reported it had dropped significantly. They called the nurse to take the blood pressure. It was only when she reported the same results that they visibly relaxed. Apparently coming from Troy, New York, was not exactly a character reference to citizens of Youngstown, Ohio. At any rate, I was now free to take care of the other patients.

The E. R. at St. Elizabeth was always filled. In this turmoil, patients were grateful for any amount of reasonable attention in a reasonable amount of waiting time. As a result, interns could perform procedures that would not have been allowed anywhere else, except perhaps city or charity hospitals. The demand for help was so great.

For the first time, we could stop acute blood flow, sew torn tendons together and close the wounds, set fractures, proudly perform cosmetic repairs of lacerations, deliver the babies that were too far along when the mothers couldn't be moved, treat acute heart attacks, counsel obvious psychiatric cases, abort impending allergic reactions, reduce blood pressures on patients who had readings that were off the scale, give ambulance medics on-the-spot training. In other words, do it all and yet have immediate back-up expertise with a quick phone call.

For a newly minted doctor, the work was the welcomed payoff after all the dry book learning, studying, and taking exams. We interns felt we were practicing medicine in heaven.

A few E. R. patients merely wanted a free warm room with three meals, so they faked symptoms. Most of these patients were not very good actors or actresses, but they were often very persistent.

One lady insisted she was blind and couldn't see. Against her wishes, I placed her in a wheel chair to wait for an open bed and offered her nothing to eat all day. At the end of eight hours, she called me some unmentionable names, miraculously recovered her eyesight, got up, and walked out unassisted.

The chaos in E. R. brings out important abilities: placing patients quickly into priority categories of those needing immediate care, those who can wait, and those who have minor problems; working rapidly; making judgments that have to be reasonably accurate, even when there's a crushing mass of shouting, emotionally upset people, especially where bleeding is involved. It becomes a challenge to soothe and add a measure of calm to the chaos, and still appreciate why the patients are upset.

E. R. doctors can order people around in a cold, callous way, or they can empathize and talk to patients understandingly. I tried to see things from the patients' view and take time, even though it meant only a moment to look them directly in the eyes, unhurriedly tell them how serious their problem was, how long it would be before I would be with them, and what I was going to do about it. It worked.

Although I've spent my life in the laboratory, my favorite place in the hospital still is the Emergency Room.

Taking care of all manner of afflictions such as cuts, bruises, headaches, sore throats, colds was a pleasure when they turned out to be just that. The pleasure was in deciding that it was *only* a cut, *only* a headache, and *only* a cold and not something more serious.

But bruises could mean decreased platelets which occur in leukemia, headaches might mean brain tumor, sore throats could mean infectious mononucleosis, and cough or a cold might mean a more serious viral infection such as early measles or whooping cough.

The early heart attacks, progressing heart attacks, early and late strokes, and all manner of devastations to the human body were most fascinating because you could do something to help.

And do it right then!

14
Specializing

14
Specializing

"**H**OW MANY PINTS OF BLOOD did you say?" the surgeon shouted. His anger was towering and his face flushed. His eyes were popping out of their sockets, and the whites shone dangerously in the dark room. "I don't see anything but a small amount of normal leakage!"

This was my first day in pathology residency—the beginning day of four years—and already I was angering one of the chief surgeons in the hospital.

Dutifully, I had begun the ordered autopsy alone in the basement of Deaconess Hospital. According to the chart, the post-surgical status of the patient slowly deteriorated over three days and he expired. The patient's family signed the authorization for a postmortem.

As soon as I opened the body cavity, I realized there was a problem with far-reaching repercussions in the surgical area of the abdomen. I phoned by boss, Dr. Haukohl, to come down to substantiate my findings before I did anything more.

Before Dr. Haukohl could come down, a chief surgeon with his three surgical residents filed into the room and loudly asked with an air of intimidation: "YOU ESTI-MATE WHAT?"

I stated as matter-as-factly and calmly as I could: "About four and a half pints of blood are in the abdominal cavity."

I answered his question after reflecting that this was a medical school professor and antagonizing him would not be the brightest thing I could do. He could be a powerful adversary who not only was a medical school faculty member, but had friends with influence.

Still, facts were facts.

The surgeon looked at his residents who were from the Philippines and were by nature non-confrontational, and yelled, "I don't see anything like that!" Looking to his residents for agreement, he questioned, "Just normal leakage, isn't it?" Without waiting for them to reply, he answered, "Of course it is normal. I've seen this hundreds of times. Every surgery has some leakage of blood! That's what you see normally."

Under his glare, I kept my face immobile.

"Where do *you* think the blood came from then?" asked the surgeon querulously.

"From the blood vessel that wasn't tied." I realized full well what I was saying, but I stood my ground.

The surgeon began to explode again.

By this time, the lab director, Dr. Haukohl, walked in. One look at our faces and he grasped the situation.

"What's the problem, Harry?"

Before I could speak, the surgeon huffed, "Well! Your

man here says there are four and a half pints of blood in the belly. That's ridiculous!"

"Is that what you estimated?" asked Dr. Haukohl looking at me.

"Yes."

"Robert—tell him he's wrong! That's normal leakage post-surgery," appealed the surgeon.

Dr. Haukohl looked into the abdominal cavity, moving the intestines from one side to the other.

He looked up at the surgeon. "Sorry, I have to agree with my resident." Dr. Haukohl then turned to me and asked, "Would you allow the amount to be closer to four pints?"

I shrugged, "Sure."

"That's what it is then. Where did you decide the blood came from?"

"Loose suture. Left renal artery," I replied.

He picked up the forceps and again moved the intestines away, so he could get a clearer view. It took about a full minute of inspection until he was satisfied.

"I agree."

Dr. Haukohl then placed the forceps on the table and walked out of the room. I was left alone with the surgeon and his minions.

"You rotten #@&*!! Two can play this game," shouted the surgeon. Turning to his residents, he blurted, "I don't ever want you to help these guys. Never help the laboratory with anything. Do you understand? Never help them with *anything*! If I catch you helping them, I'll . . . I'll . . ."

He stumbled for the words.

The surgical residents looked down at the floor and at the ceiling. When the surgeon stormed out with his residents following, one resident hung back and whispered to me. "We told him the patient was bleeding internally, but he refused to believe us or let us do anything."

I don't know if the surgeon had performed other procedures that were inadequate; but when my preliminary autopsy findings were reported, the surgeon immediately lost his surgical and hospital privileges, and shortly thereafter, his professorship. Three months after that, he retired from practicing medicine.

I came up from the autopsy room and looked into Dr. Haukohl's office. "There's a lot more to the practice of pathology than I thought," I said.

"Yes."

"I thought all I had to do was set up tests, interpret results, and diagnose tissue biopsies. No one told me I had to be a policeman too."

He had a wry smile on his face. "So you learned something."

"So . . . ," I carefully phrased my thoughts, "I'm going to make some people very angry about what I honestly find and report. I didn't expect *this*."

Dr. Haukohl lit an unfiltered Camel, took a deep drag, and blew out the smoke. "It's worse than you think. If you're going to be a pathologist, you'll have to get used to being like Caesar's wife. You must be 'above suspicion.'

How does the quote go? 'I wish my wife to be not so much as suspected.'"

I grimaced in agreement. "Why didn't they teach us this in school?"

Dr. Haukohl lifted an eyebrow and gave me a lopsided smile. "There's a lot to learn outside of school, isn't there?"

Well, if that wasn't enough to begin my pathology residency, the next day I accompanied Dr. Haukohl upstairs to surgery for a frozen-section consultation. He was handed a piece of tissue that was barely visible on the gauze. He glanced at it, threw it down, and banged open the surgical doors.

"How big is the tumor?" he demanded.

The surgeon mumbled something back that we couldn't hear.

"The size of a grapefruit?" Dr. Haukohl continued.

There was more mumbling from the surgeon.

"The size of an orange then?" queried Dr. Haukohl undeterred.

The surgeon nodded reluctantly.

"Then give me a piece I can work with!" insisted Dr. Haukohl with no attempt to hide his disgust.

After a short wait, the scrub nurse handed us a piece of gauze with tissue about the size of a walnut. Dr. Haukohl froze the tissue to cut it. After staining it, he looked at it under the microscope.

With the result, he banged open the surgical doors and dramatically announced, "It's malignant."

As we walked downstairs, I asked, "Why didn't he

give us a decent piece of tumor tissue the first time when there was so much of it?"

"Games. Surgeons play games."

"All of them?"

"No. Just the #@&*!! with big egos. It kills them not to know when a swelling is cancer or not. They don't have the training, so they try to jab the pathologist who does know. Don't worry. You'll know the guys with the black and white hats right away."

Every day for a week, I practiced doing frozen sections on fresh tissues. I couldn't wait for a call from surgery to show off my accomplishment to the laboratory director.

"Surgery wants you," called a secretary.

Dr. Haukohl and I walked upstairs together. He was handed a piece of breast tissue about the size of a pea. I expected him to ask for a larger piece. Instead, he barely glanced down at it, opened the doors of surgery, and yelled, "Malignant!" He turned and walked away.

"Wait!" I shouted, alarmed. "It's so small. Aren't you going to freeze it and confirm it?"

"Why bother? It's malignant."

"But . . . but how do you know for sure?" I was shocked and thought to myself: "My God! He barely examined it! What kind of teacher did I pick? This is scary."

Dr. Haukohl fixed on me with stern, forbidding eyes. "If you can't tell breast malignancy in two weeks by looking at it as I did, you'll no longer be *my* resident. You can go into something easier to learn. Like surgery."

I looked for some sort of line in his face that meant he was jesting. There was none. He *meant* it!

If I didn't learn to do what he just did, with absolute accuracy, I was going to be thrown out of my residency. A doctor couldn't say something was cancer, unless he knew it for certain. That meant *total, complete* certainty. I had just started in this specialized field. He'd been a pathologist for years and years. How could I do what he just did? That seemed so unfair.

Unfair or not, I carefully inspected all gross tissue specimens that I could find in our hospital lab, and read book after book. I went to Milwaukee County Hospital, Columbia Hospital, St. Mary's Hospital, every hospital laboratory where I knew a fellow resident, and asked to see any gross specimens of breast biopsies. Learning all I could, I even received some extra tissue that I could take with me and examine.

At the end of two weeks, Dr. Haukohl stopped by the resident's cubicle. "How are you coming with diagnosing malignant breast tissue grossly?"

"Good," I answered cautiously.

"*Good*? 'Good' is not good enough," he said crossly. "Write out at least a full page, single-spaced, of the gross description of a malignant breast tissue and bring it to me right away."

So I did. I wrote: *There are multiple different types of breast cancer, the most common being scirrhous carcinoma or duct cell type, which has many other names. One chief characteristic to look for in gross inspection is hardness of the tissue. It is almost rock-hard and is quite different from the surrounding breast stroma. The malignant tumor is almost always irregular in shape and extends into the surrounding supporting tissue fat with pseudopodia often demonstrating a haphazard arrangement. No definite capsule is suggested. The surface presents a dirty-gray or gray-white appearance. Often, but not necessarily, small chalky spots are present consisting of calcific deposits. The calcific areas are often visible on X-ray. Such areas are always suspicious in any breast biopsy. When cutting into the scirrhous type of carcinoma, one feels a gritty sensation to the knife edge . . . .*

I continued on about other cancers of the breast to finish the writing assignment.

After reading the summary, Dr. Haukohl looked up without expression. "Let's see if you can lift all this off the paper and use it in surgery. I want you to see the calcium with those X-ray eyes that you put in this description."

In the succeeding weeks, we went to surgery together and each time he handed me the surgical specimen, asking me for a diagnosis. I was able to diagnose the gross specimens correctly with more and more confidence partly because, after he left, I froze part of every surgical tissue anyway and looked at it through the microscope.

Even though I had given the correct diagnosis, I felt better comparing the appearance of the fresh gross tissue with the appearance under the microscope immediately, rather than after it was fixed in formalin and processed that afternoon. Formalin fixation shrinks tissues about 10% and the characteristic landmarks, stained in fresh tissue, are often quite different from those of fixed tissue under the microscope.

After a few months, the loudspeaker blared: "Pathologist needed in surgery right away!"

Before I could even start to get up, Dr. Haukohl stepped into the resident's room and barked, "Didn't you hear the call? They want a pathologist in surgery right away."

Up to now, the routine had been for him, on the run, to shout, "Let's go, Harry!" over his shoulder. But this time, he showed no indication that he was going with me.

Mouth agape, I started to say something, but he interrupted with an irritated wave of his hand. "Move! Get up there!" he yelled. "The patient is under anesthesia, and the whole operating room is waiting for *you*!"

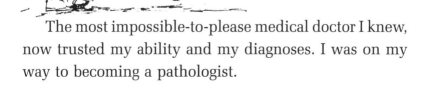

I leaped out of my chair and when out of his sight, did a happy, double-time walk and, while in the elevator, bounced out a few tap-dance steps as it traveled up to the fifth floor. There was joy in every stride to surgery.

The most impossible-to-please medical doctor I knew, now trusted my ability and my diagnoses. I was on my way to becoming a pathologist.

15

Pacific Northwest

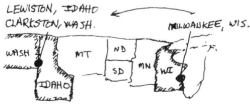

LEWISTON, IDAHO
CLARKSTON, WASH.

MILWAUKEE, WIS.

15
Pacific Northwest

IT WAS MY GOOD FORTUNE, during residency at St. Mary's, to work with a fine doctor, Carl Koenen, who decided he wanted to practice in the West. We formed a partnership and began, during the fourth year of residency, to investigate openings for pathologists in the Pacific Northwest.

We wrote to everyone we knew out West, using the College of American Pathologists' list of available openings. Also, we checked with the American Society of Clinical Pathologists who had councilors in every state and whose purpose was to assist newly graduated pathologists. We wrote to those who were responsible for Idaho, Washington, Oregon, Utah, and Montana.

Each weekend, the one who was off duty flew to check out listed openings. After investigating some openings, Carl and I concluded that we didn't care to be in a salaried position on a large hospital pathology staff with little or no job security, no matter how prestigious. And we didn't appreciate our present position where the two of us did all the work and the Chief Pathologist spent all his time elsewhere. Both took unfair advantage of newly graduated physician-pathologists. Clearly then, we wanted to be on our own and build up our own practice. Carl finished his residency six months before I did and marked time by working on the staff at St. Mary's while we investigated different openings.

Almost as soon as we made the decision to go it alone and not join any group, we received a brief line from Dr. Don Merkeley of Lewiston, Idaho, stating he was leaving to practice in Seattle. It was my turn to travel and check out any openings.

I realized, in the first hour of my arrival in Lewiston, that this was the place. The people in the valley who lived at the confluence of the Snake and Clearwater Rivers seemed wonderful. I returned and got Carl to come to Lewiston with me, hopefully to agree with my choice.

Even though there was only enough work for one doctor, we were impressed with two things about the laboratory: (1) it was accredited by the American Society of Clinical Pathologists, which made it first class; and (2) Dr. Merkeley had established the first and only blood bank in Idaho. This particularly interested us since the Milwaukee Blood Bank, one of the best in the nation, had been our training ground. And if a small town like Lewiston supported the only independent blood bank in the entire state, it had to have tremendous community spirit.

After meeting some of the citizens, our impressions were confirmed. The Lewiston, Idaho / Clarkston, Washington, area had the finest people we had ever met—not only that, they were genuinely friendly, amusing, and enjoyed playing tricks on each other.

We were to meet friends like Hurley H. where I learned expressions like "He had a lot of trouble cornering the truth."

We were to meet Bob L. and Bill L., who named his dog "Hurley" just so Bill could say the most awful things to the dog every time Hurley came to visit. Hurley never did see the humor in that, but it broke us all up when Bill would say to his dog, "Hurley, you're the laziest, dumbest, godforsaken excuse for anything I've ever seen."

 We were to meet France R., who had more horses than his wife knew about. It was a treat to ask him, in front of his wife, how many horses he owned and watch him stutter and try to explain he didn't really know.

We were to meet Jim G. who took off his cowboy boots and gave them to me when he learned I didn't own a pair. "Not allowed!" he said. "Not allowed to live in Lewiston without owning a pair of genuine boots!"

Bill McC. and Reed C. were good for any number of practical jokes. One of Reed's best was getting two round pieces of sponge and covering them with frosting, like a cake, and placing candles on it for a birthday party. France was almost in tears at being so thoughtfully remembered until he tried and tried to cut the "cake."

We were to meet Lou G. whose many expressions I've used including one of his descriptions of a race horse he disliked. "He's got a heart the size of a pea." Somehow, that said it all.

As for the physicians, never had we met so many eccentric but compatible doctors, especially when we were greeted by an "Englishman" who wore a bowling ball hat and affected an English accent the entire time.

Carl and I passed the State Boards in Medicine in Idaho and Washington, and then successfully completed the College of American Pathologists' Specialty Boards in Anatomic as well as Clinical Pathology. We officially started medical practice and never once regretted our choice in selecting the wonderful Lewis-Clark Valley. We had found home.

The only major problem was resolving who was the *senior* pathologist. Carl started in August, 1963, and I began January, 1964. He insisted he was the senior because of his longer time in pathology practice in Lewiston, and I demanded seniority because of my advanced age. "Older is better because older is wiser," I told him, but he resisted accepting the irrefutable logic of this truism.

Thirty-two years later and this important issue is still not resolved.

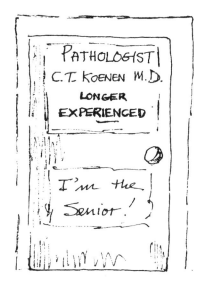 

16

merry
Mary

16
Merry
Mary

COLORADO WAS THE BEST CHOICE I ever made because I met Mary there. She was so comfortable and easy to be with that I thought I had known her all my life. I don't know what she saw in me back then and I guess I'll never know because each time I ask her, she laughs and laughs.

Since Mary loves horses so, I often wonder if horses and I have something in common.

After meeting Mary, I became more serious about doing something productive and accepting responsibility because, after graduating from the University of Colorado, I asked Mary to marry me.

Merry Mary said, "Yes."

It was clearly not a responsible thing to do since I still had five years of medical school and internship, and four more school years after that if I wanted to specialize. What if children came? How would we support ourselves?

I had no money, no prospects, and no family enterprise to fall back on.

Strangely, during my entire life, I never felt that the lack of money was a drawback for not doing something. Perhaps it was because at an early age, in the grocery store, I handled lots of money and saw it come and go. Money generally means little if your wants are few. My wants had been few and my thoughts, if anything, were mostly naive, philosophical ones. Still, there was always the unjustified but blind belief that I'd somehow succeed. Starting from nothing simply took a little longer.

Mary felt the same way. How did I ever find such a wonderful girl who had such faith and confidence?

In August, 1952, Mary Corcoran from Milwaukee, Wisconsin, actually married me with only one request: that we would return to the West as soon as medical school was finished.

That summer I worked in construction. But after Mary and I got married, we moved to Rochester, New York, the next day. We had only enough money for tuition so we found the cheapest accommodations—a small, airless, dingy basement apartment. She began work as a receptionist in Strong Memorial Hospital.

By necessity, we had to exist on her weekly salary which, after taxes, ended up around $23. A fringe benefit with her job was a free evening meal at the hospital. I accompanied her and ate from her tray. The food handlers reported us and tried to stop it, but after an appeal to the hospital administrator, it was allowed. This was often our only meal for the day.

In January, Mary became pregnant. We were very

happy, even though it was (once again) not a responsible thing to do. We moved to a larger apartment for the same amount of rent. It was an easy move: our furniture consisted of orange crates for chairs, planks and bricks for bookshelves, and a bed.

Our experiences at Rochester, New York, were mostly bad, except for meeting and learning from Dr. George Whipple, Nobel Prize winner and pathologist. So we returned to Milwaukee. Through Mary's careful budgeting and her parents' help, we managed to recoup and she helped me earn a Master of Science and Doctorate in Medicine from Marquette University. This was followed by a splendid rotating internship at St. Elizabeth's in Youngstown, Ohio; passing the Wisconsin State Board of Medicine licensing exam; and returning to Milwaukee to begin a residency in pathology.

The learning experience in becoming a good doctor was marvelous, *unbelievably* marvelous. But the hours— 24 on and 24 off—were ghastly. The emotional drain was so complete that afterwards the only desire was for sleep, even though I tried to share as many of these wonderful experiences as I could with my Mary who was home with our children.

All successful men, not just physicians, are able to stay focused on their jobs because their wives put up with hours of lost companionship. Their dedication is, in many ways, much harder. Luckily for me, Mary was aware of the long road we had chosen because her mother was a nurse and her father a physician.

Still, even being aware of the empty time to come, is different from actually experiencing it. There's the minimum of four years of undergraduate work, four years of medical school, the year of internship, and yet to come is the specialization, usually four more years. It's a lonely life for someone married to a beginning physician, and it's an unusual person who can cope with this loneliness. The lost time together, when you are young and vibrant, is gone forever. *Nie Kehrst Du Wieder, Goldene Zeit.*

The true heroines are wives.

17
Failing

17
Failing

I REALLY WANTED TO BE LIKE UNCLE AGOPENNY and tell stories like he did, but it didn't work out because he had the knack and I didn't. Any stories I told must have made people wonder because they never laughed or smiled or said anything. I failed no matter how I practiced. It didn't take long to realize that I could try until doomsday and still not come near to what Uncle Agopenny could do naturally.

Over the years, I've heard a lot of people talk and give accounts of incidents, even ones that were very simple, and they kept everyone interested in every word they said. I enjoyed the talk very much and it was only afterwards, when I couldn't remember much of exactly *what* was said, that I realized that some people had the storytelling gift. Maybe you won't agree it's a gift, but by calling it a gift, I feel better about not being able to do it.

When I finally figured out that I wasn't ever going to be much good at talking, I picked writing as being closest to talking, without actually talking. What's more, I figured if I threw in a drawing or two, who knows, maybe the readers wouldn't notice the roughness in the writing so much.

So in the third year of high school, I began writing in earnest and submitted essays to Mr. Howell at Troy High School. He was head of the English Department and was in charge of literature and writing, both fiction and non-fiction. He was also known for being a hard grader and never giving A's. Even though my grades weren't much, I thought I was doing very well because he picked me for an important part in a play. I tried very hard to please him by volunteering for everything he suggested to our class.

What I liked about Mr. Howell was the way he ran up to the teacher's lounge between classes and had a snort of whiskey. It made him so human and, well, likable because he was breaking the rules. He'd come down after ten minutes and begin talking about the classics in the wonderful loud, raspy voice that he had. For the next fifty minutes, he took us out of Troy, New York, and put us in elegant England.

As he talked, he would recite poetry and read stories

like we never heard them before. He'd wipe the tears from his eyes when he laughed and he'd wipe the tears from his eyes when he cried—all without the slightest shame. He was so awesome. I would have given him a barrel of whiskey, if that's what he needed to perform so well for us unappreciative, ignorant kids.

On the last day of school, after we had all lined up in English class to say our good-byes to the teacher, it came my turn. I started to thank Mr. Howell and tell him how much I enjoyed his class. Instead, he glanced at me briefly, stuck out a wet fish of a hand, and said, "Mr. Chinchinian, you've been a disappointment to me." Abruptly, he went on to the next student with a smile and a cheerful word.

It bothered me a lot, even though I was used to this kind of treatment—after all, as a member of Antranik's gang, nice people had good reason to avoid us and say bad things about us. Still, I would have liked Mr. Howell to have said I was a *major* disappointment, or an especially *sad* disappointment, or said something really *bad* that I had done. At least, that way, you see, I'd be outstanding and would have achieved something. But to be only labeled "a disappointment," well, I felt he was telling me he never thought I'd amount to much anyway and wasn't worth spending any time on.

It seemed that failure was something I would have to learn to live with regularly.

Math did not come easily, so I took the same courses over and over again. Foreign languages were a struggle; pronouncing the words was hard, and I made a thousand mistakes before I could come close to being understood.

Football in high school was a lot of fun, but the coach compared me to Antranik's cousin. He'd say, "Why can't you be like Duke? You're Armenian, aren't you?" Unlike me, Duke was so tough that you just gave him the ball and he ran it down the field with two or three guys hanging on him.

I didn't pass the Senior Life Guard exam and had to try again. I failed the first test of Water Safety Instructor, and had to go back and try again. And try again. I failed my driver's license test, and not just once.

I had a passion for snow skiing which started in Middlebury, Vermont, and increased in Switzerland. I did nothing but fall in every possible manner. A total klutz.

Later in life, was horseback riding. The first dozen times were disasters. I know they were disasters because my daughter told me to get off her horse forever, before I ruined the animal. She was eleven years old and knew better.

Still, the hardest failure to accept was failing at writing because it made me also stop drawing. In my mind, and I know it doesn't make sense, I had them mixed together. Somehow I couldn't do one without the other.

So you see, I'm sort of a champion at failing. I've failed at so many things that I could win the World Championship in Failing. But I told myself it didn't matter. I expected it, allowed for it, and kept plugging away. Failure was a mad dog chasing me and I just had to outrun it.

I kept recalling how Pop kept coming to America. He

failed to get in six times and would have tried six *times* seven if he had to. I must have inherited some of his stubbornness because I also kept on trying, kept running like mad to achieve, in spite of failing.

Well, what finally happened was that I did get to play football, even if I drove the coach nuts. I did receive an instructor's certificate in Red Cross Water Safety, and I did pass the driver's license exam. I was able to speak French and German after going to school in several foreign countries. I did, eventually, learn to ski well enough to get on the regular ski patrol at Winter Park, Colorado. I even got to go to medical school and practice medicine, and become a college professor. But of all the achievements, I should be proudest was being able to sit on a horse and not interfere with what it wanted to do. So much so, that once, in my lifetime, my daughter allowed me to ride her horse in a parade all by myself.

As for the writing and drawing, it wasn't until my mother-in-law, Mrs. Corcoran, whom I adored from the moment I met her, called me on the phone and said, "I've just turned 80 years old and did you know that when you reach 80 years, you can command people to do whatever you want and they have to do it?"

I replied I hadn't heard of that rule but if she said it existed, then it must be so, and I would be delighted to be commanded by her.

"Well," she said, "my wish is that you write me a letter once a week."

"That's it? Something as dumb and easy as that? What would you like me to write about?"

"You'll find something," she answered and couldn't be persuaded to say any more.

So I started writing and drawing about twelve years ago, because after all, it *was* a command and commands are not things one should take lightly.

Well, since Mrs. Corcoran had been out West, going to horse shows and meeting lots of our friends and enjoying the pioneers who homesteaded this area and the area around Joseph Creek, there was always something interesting, funny, and unbelievable to write to her about. When you live in the Lewis-Clark Valley, you can easily start out each letter with the words, "You won't believe this, but here goes . . . "

Soon there were hundreds of letters, all filled with stories and drawings about animals and people. Mary and our three children figured in all of this and rounded out each letter.

In the past few years, I begged off, asking my mother-in-law to suspend her command temporarily, so that I could write something other than letters. The terms of her release were: "As long as I get to read it." This release, or shall I say command, gave me more time to write stories.

Life has so many twists and turns, doesn't it? What happens is often not what you start out to do. Then it twists and turns again, so that you *do* end up with what you started and wanted to do.

Well, life isn't fair or predictable so you take the good with the bad. As the saying goes, you play the cards the way they are dealt.

That's why, when all is said and done, just look at how, in this crazy, wonderful life, you can fail and fail and fail and still *win*.

18
Teachers

18

Teachers

"THAT DUMB SUBJECT? How can you ever like that?"
"Don't take chemistry. It's too hard!"

Do you remember how you thought chemistry or math or English or some other class was boring or too hard, and then a teacher came along who made it fascinating? Only because of this terrific teacher, the course ended up great. And then, each time that subject came up, the memory of that teacher came with it, along with good feelings and useful knowledge.

The good teachers inspire and teach with dignity and care. They make school a place of fun. And because it is fun, learning becomes easy and a pleasure, and because it is a pleasure, the knowledge stays longer and is used more.

Sometimes the teacher does nothing more than tell you to forget some confusing part because it isn't really important: "The part that you really should know well is right here."

What a difference that bit of help and guidance makes!

Other times the teacher encourages you not to quit: "It's not so hard. Here. Repeat it after me."

You try and it comes out poorly.

"*Wonderful!* That was just *wonderful!* Would you do that again for me?"

You don't think it was so good; in fact, you think it was awful, but you try it again and again and then once more because of the teacher.

And the teacher smiles, pats you on the back. "You are going to do well. Very well."

With that, you puff out your chest and feel ten feet tall. When you go home and practice, it goes well. Very well. Just like the teacher said it would be. It *is* better! You can't *believe* it! It's amazing!

If it is a time in your life when you are being dumped on repeatedly, then you will especially remember every word of encouragement from teachers. It won't matter how old you get. You'll always remember.

I know I remember that no matter how bad things got, there was always a teacher somewhere who had a kind word for me.

I'm sure you remember that special teacher who believed in *you*—the one who helped you when no one else bothered? Perhaps you were lucky and had more than one. I did.

In fact, I had many, many good teachers. The three

who meant the most to me were the violin teacher Mr. Catricala, the pathology professor Dr. Whipple, and the internal medicine resident Dr. Joe. Their inspiration helped me through some hard times, especially when failure was chasing me.

As for failing, I mean as for the *bright* side of failing, and there is *always* a bright side, I developed a sympathy for those who didn't grasp things right away.

So when I myself became a teacher, I remembered what it was like to be in the shoes of a failing student and knew firsthand how exhausting it was not to understand something after trying and trying.

The exhaustion of trying and failing is as much mental as it is physical. So as a teacher, I couldn't laugh and joke about it, but could honestly sympathize and say, "I've been there and this is how I licked it . . . . If I can do it, so can you."

If it didn't make me a *better* teacher, then at least it made me a very *patient* one.

To a child, the teacher is the steady life-line in a cold, uncaring, stormy ocean. Everyone needs someone and a young immigrant kid like me, with no means and no background, especially needed teachers who believed in him and would take the time to help him.

And the teachers were there . . . teachers who inspired and taught with dignity and care, because that's the way they saw their real job.

At life's end, there may be a Dwelling up there where we eventually go to rest. As we each apply and state our occupations, I know that a lot of good, dedicated people who say, "I was a teacher" will get a very special place.

I know this for certain because in all of life, there is *absolutely, absolutely* nothing as wonderful as a caring teacher.

Absolutely nothing.

About the Author

Harry Chinchinian, whose parents were Armenian immigrants, was born the younger of two sons in Troy, New York.

All illustrations, appearing in Book One and Book Two of *Immigrant Son*, were drawn by the author; several are the original sketches from over 50 years ago.

His interest in storytelling and illustrating goes back to childhood. The playful style in his writing and drawings reflects an uncanny refusal to grow up.